S. SEKOU ABODUNRIN

MANIFESTING ANSWERS TO
PRAYERS
Transforming answers to experiences

SEKOU
PUBLISHING

Manifesting Answers To Prayers
Transforming answers to experiences

Sekou Publishing sekou@sekou.me
Copyright © 2015 by Sekou Abodunrin
ISBN: 978-0-9575677-4-0
Published by Sekou Publishing. All rights reserved.

Cover Design and Page Layout
Kenteba Kreations
www.kentebakreations.com

So you have taken the bold step to find out what happened to all those texts of yours that never got delivered? That's brilliant, you are not alone. The Pharaoh of Egypt faced the same dilemma thousands of years ago. Really? Just kidding. Anyway, I know you are too smart to take advice about missing texts from him. But Hey! Keep surfing within these pages and you just might find an explanation.

CONTENTS

INTRODUCTION

It would appear that the only thing in as much plentiful supply to the prayer of the saints is that we don't have more books that teach how to execute the basics of prayer, so that we can have more successful prayer lives.

For those countless hours of praying that I cannot trace out manifestations of answers for, I have learnt not to put up barriers between my Father God and I. This is written for those who want to know what our responsibilities are after God answers our prayer. The principles discussed mostly address the prayer of faith.

Prayer is seeing so much of Christ that you are no longer hypnotized by the make-belief of this earth's sphere. Prayer is fighting from victory and not for victory. It is coming under the hypnosis of God's love. God is not tag-teaming with satan to keep your prayer life in check. God and satan are not on the same team. God already said yes to all the benefits in Christ but satan takes advantage of ignorance in Christians. He camouflages as God in order to prevent our enjoyment of the answers that God has given. It is our aim that in these pages you come to a Christ-entranced vision of prayer. And by so doing, you discover a more Christ-like God.

And it shall come to pass, that before they call, I will answer; and while they are yet speaking, I will hear.
Isaiah 65:24

APPRECIATION

This that you hold in your hands is a result of many years as a student at the feet of teachers whose clarity of thought has sparked within me a divine hunger and a healthy appetite for thinking and exploring in God.

I am grateful for the members of GracePlace and the people who listen to my holy ramblings as I try to articulate and simplify the communication of the thoughts and principles within this book.

To all those wonderful folks who enrich me by bringing me out of my brain and into my senses, you help me live in the here and now – Alex Emiola and Alfreda Adunola.

1

PRAYING FOR OTHERS

Let my prayer be set forth before thee as incense; and the lifting up of my hands as the evening sacrifice.
Psalm 141:2

God definitely hears prayer but when prayer becomes praise and thanksgiving God also smells our prayer. When we pray from a consciousness of what Christ has accomplished, it is the purest perfume in the nostrils of God. Prayer is like you and God sniffing Christ and hitting a high together for Christ is the substance and fragrance of real prayer.

There are realms in prayer that open up only as we learn to pray for others.

Don't succumb to condemnation

As people sow to their flesh satan takes advantage of their sense of guilt and condemnation. He hopes that they reap corruption (Gal. 6:8). He knows that he is no match for the mercy of God, which we put into operation when we pray for others. He therefore needs us to give up hope that our prayers are positively influencing their transformation. He provides the conviction that there is no use praying since he wants us to think that we started praying too late. He might even accuse you that you are part of the reason why that loved one has turned out badly. He needs you to succumb to condemnation – don't!

Some perish, others are spared

Satan wanted to sift Peter (See Lk. 22:31-33), just like he had sifted Job. Jesus prayed that Peter's faith would not fail. Since Faith is the victory that overcomes the world faith can never fail (1 John 5:4). It was Peter who did not resist satan by faith. Peter's unbelief stopped him from reaping the victory contained within faith. Faith didn't fail, Peter failed. Faith was stored up in Peter as a result of hearing Jesus' sermons over time. Jesus trusted that the Word would work to restore Peter, so He prayed for Peter.

Jesus told Peter to still fill his position of leadership once he repented. Jesus anticipated repentance because He had supplied the power for recovery to Peter through His prayers. After praying for Peter, Jesus gave him hope concerning what lay ahead. This hope likely bailed Peter out of his personal tribulation after he denied Jesus. Jesus' prayer was all that stood between Peter and suicide. Otherwise out of condemnation, Peter might have committed suicide like Judas did. Peter acted on the power supplied through Jesus' prayer for him, got back on his feet and became a pillar in the Church (Gal. 2:9).

Why didn't Peter commit suicide like Judas?

Jesus shed some light on this when His disciples wanted to know why Pilate murdered some Galileans and others were not. Jesus said people don't die prematurely because they were worse sinners than others. Other factors come into play and He used a parable to communicate His answer.

> *He spake also this parable; A certain man had a fig tree planted in his vineyard; and he came and sought fruit thereon, and found none. Then said he unto the dresser of his vineyard, Behold, these three years I come seeking fruit on this fig tree, and find none: cut it down; why cumbereth it the ground? And he answering said unto him, Lord, let it alone this year also, till I shall dig about it, and dung it: And if it bear fruit, well: and if not, then after that thou shalt cut it down.*
> *Luke 13:6-9*

In this parable, God is the owner of the vineyard. The fig tree represents Israel. Jesus was the dresser of the vineyard who obtained extension of mercy in the hope that the nation of Israel would repent. Jesus' intercession caused a delay of judgment. If they remained barren, they would reap being "cut off".

We come across people who, like that fig tree, resist bearing fruit. We as the body of Christ act as channels of compassion and exercise our authority to execute mercy over the errant one. We provide safety for that person using mercy as a weapon to push back destruction. While destruction is delayed the person has the chance to bear the fruit of repentance. In that sense those who have no one praying for them have nothing to slow down their being "cut down". As we pray for our loved ones we must act like our prayers are working by continually praising God for the change taking place in them. We actively believe for the ministry of angels to preserve their physical life from harm.

People have been encouraged to think God is the problem when they have heard religious people tell them, "God is mad at you because you did such and such a thing". When the church speaks this way it becomes the avenue through which people become blinded to God's true nature. We think we are teaching holiness whereas we are just blinding people to the reconciliation that God has provided in Christ. If you don't want to have to pray the prayer of intercession for your kids when they grow up, stop telling them in their childhood years that God is mad at them when they are naughty. Speak God's blessing over them because Jesus is the basis of mercy.

We don't intercede because God is angry but because when people persist in sin God does not hold back His mercy, instead it is people that forsake their own mercies! (Jonah 2:8). People are sowing and reaping satanic destruction. When interceding we thank God profusely because He freely shows mercy because Jesus is the propitiation for all sin (1 John 2:2).

On the other hand people who are blinded by satan cooperate with satan to co-create calamity for themselves and for others. Someone needs to stand in between people and the alliance they have formed with satan through ignorance.

The prayer that we pray to suspend the advantage satan has over people through ignorance and blindness is the prayer of intercession. They are sowing to the flesh and reaping judgment. Through intercession we are holding back the judgment that men draw upon themselves because of their blind minds..

The redemption that we have in Christ Jesus has radically changed the nature of intercession. The Old Testament saints did not have Jesus, however in the day of the New Covenant we do. Therefore the way Moses, Abraham and the Old Testament saints prayed and the way we pray the prayer of intercession are radically different. Though people sinned then, and they still sin today, there is a big difference – His name is Jesus.

The Bible contains examples of intercessors before Jesus came.

Abraham was a limited Mediator

And the LORD said, Because the cry of Sodom and Gomorrah is great, and because their sin is very grievous; I will go down now, and see whether they have done altogether according to the cry of it, which is come unto me; and if not, I will know. And the men turned their faces from thence, and went toward Sodom: but Abraham stood yet before the LORD. And Abraham drew near, and said, Wilt thou also destroy the righteous with the wicked? Peradventure there be fifty righteous within the city: wilt thou also destroy and not spare the place for the fifty righteous that are therein? That be far from thee to do after this manner, to slay the righteous with the wicked: and that the righteous should be as the wicked, that be far from thee: Shall not the Judge of all the earth do right? And the LORD said, If I find in Sodom fifty righteous within the city, then I will spare all the place for their sakes. And he said, Oh let not the LORD be angry, and I will speak yet but this once: Peradventure ten shall be found there. And he said, I will not destroy it for ten's sake.
Genesis 18:20,23-26, 32

Sin confuses men; there is nothing good about it. As you read this story you cannot help but notice that even though a city is sinful, God will spare that city for the sake of those who are His. Abraham did not catch that hint. God later showed Ezekiel that he would spare a city for the sake of one man who makes up the hedge! (Ezek. 22:30). We should not be looking for reasons why a city should be destroyed, but how to preserve them in order that they might hear the Gospel and respond in faith.

In order to understand this story, remember that God gave man authority on the earth (Gen. 1:26). Man is the one that authorizes good or bad spirits to work on this earth. In Eden, God did not create thorns. It was Adam's actions that caused the earth to produce thorns (Gen. 3:18). By cooperating with satan, Adam had sown violence into the earth and the earth revolted.

In Abraham's day, a spiritual cry rose out of Sodom because men had saturated the earth with violence. It was a cry for judgment. It was like thick, dark rain clouds gathering just before it rains. Man's action was cooperating with satan and shrinking God's protective presence on earth while giving satan access to steal, kill and destroy.

In His mercy God was looking to use Abraham's authority to rescue Sodom by withholding judgment. God wanted to use the intercession of Abraham to bring God's protective presence to spare that land. The citizens of Sodom had by their sin and unbelief cooperated with satan and banished God's protective presence and given place to the devil who wrecked havoc and wiped out Sodom. If Sodom had repented, their repentance would have increased the footprint of God's protective presence (Ezek. 33:11). Satan is unable to kill and destroy in an atmosphere of faith.

God does not decide which lands to spare and which to destroy. Man is the variable. Sometimes man uses his God-given authority and through intercession invites the protective presence of God. At other times man does not take his place. God is always looking for a man (Ezek. 22:30). Jesus is the basis for God's mercy, not our intercession. Intercession wears down the cooperation men supply to satan.

Abraham did not understand God's true nature. Abraham did not know that God loved the whole world and would go to any length for the salvation of one soul. In his intercession, he did not once ask for God's mercy! He had limited understanding of how to function as intercessor. Abraham was unsure as to how right God would be in His dealings. He wrongly assumed that God could find ten righteous people in Sodom. Abraham could only intercede on the natural plane. None of the conditions he gave God could be met. He did not even remember Lot. Thankfully God did. In God's merciful provision, nothing could happen until Lot was safe (Gen. 19:22).

Jesus is the greater intercessor who obtained redemption for the whole world, though Abraham failed at sparing Sodom.

Moses was also a limited Mediator

Moses functioned as a mediator (Gal. 3:19). Moses often begged God not to destroy the people. God is not the adversary trying to destroy man. Satan is. Moses did not know these facts. You don't find much information about satan in the writings of Moses apart from the serpent tempting Eve in the garden. Based on his limited understanding, he saw God as the adversary who could destroy the people because they provoked Him.

Turn from thy fierce wrath, and repent of this evil against thy people.
Exodus 32:12b

Moses felt that God's will was wrath. Therefore he prayed for God's will to be suspended. We now know that God is not willing that any should perish (2 Pet. 3:9). It would be incorrect to tell God to turn from His fierce wrath! New Testament prayer does not get God to alter His will. It gets us to alter ours, so that we come into alignment with God. Jesus prayed, "Your will be done on earth" (Mt. 6:10). Not once did Jesus ask that God repent of His planned evil as Moses prayed (Ex. 32:12). Jesus saw no need to change God's will. He prayed to release it. Jesus never attempted to change God's mind, He was the revelation of it. We don't really understand intercession, by studying intercessions in the Old Testament. We understand intercession, by understanding Jesus the Intercessor. We are to pray like Jesus, not like Moses. We pray for men today but we are conscious of the key New Testament fact that just as there is only one God, Jesus is also the only intercessor (1 Tim. 2:5).

The reason for the extensive destructions in the Old Testament was neither due to those people being worse sinners nor have anything to do with God having anger issues. There just was no man to function as intercessor to delay the reaping of the harvest of unbelief (Isaiah 59:16). Solomon concluded that it was better to be dead than alive under that setup (Eccl. 4:1-3). This is why God gave us Jesus the righteous one (1 Jn. 2:1). Now that we have an Intercessor and the power of the new nature, power is no longer on the side of the oppressor! We should expect a different outcome in our day because there is a man in heaven at the right hand of God, who releases supernatural power as He prays through the church on earth. Believers who do not understand this change that happened at the ushering in of the New Testament are trying to be intercessors supposedly holding back the fierce wrath of God. They are backing up the wrong tree however because God is not looking for a way to condemn men. God is looking for a way to get people to see what Christ has accomplished and to walk in the knowledge of it.

Yielding to Jesus the Intercessor

Our effectiveness in praying for others in the New Testament is directly linked to our understanding how to cooperate with the compassion of Jesus who is the Intercessor. Jesus is not the best intercessor He is the only intercessor. Any prayer of intercession must stay conscious of this. We are not standing between God and men trying to talk God out of sending calamity. God is not out to destroy your loved one in the first instance even if they have sinned; therefore your prayers cannot stop Him from doing so. We are not even telling God to show mercy! Jesus is the mercy of God. We are standing between men and their reaping the harvests of unbelief. We are weakening their cooperation with the destroyer who steals and kills. We are combating the blindness in the heart of men so that they can receive the light of God's Word (2 Cor. 4:3).

We cannot use prayer alone to achieve what the Lord has said is to be achieved through His Word, for God saves through the foolishness of preaching (1 Cor. 1:18). How demons must love it that we keep waiting for a move of God not realizing that we are the move of God! The truth is that Jesus is stirring us by His Word and His Spirit to act as His body and His men on the earth. We are the embodiment of Christ. We are the embodiment of power. We are to heal the sick, preach the Word and be the light of our world.

Wherefore he is able also to save them to the uttermost that come unto God by him, seeing he ever liveth to make intercession for them.
Hebrews 7:25

Jesus is now the mediator between God and man because He is also a man. Jesus is in Heaven, not on the earth. All the prayers that men prayed in the Bible were prayed from the earth because the earth is man's dominion. The intercession that Jesus makes is forever. This intercession is the life that He lives for us as the representative man in the heavens, the Head of the Church. When Jesus needs to pray as the Intercessor, He cannot do so in Heaven for Heaven is not man's dominion. He is touched with the feelings of our infirmities – the infirmity of blindness and ignorance. He shares these feelings as burdens that men on the earth pray off. It is important to understand this. Jesus prays through you as you yield in love to His Spirit within your reborn spirit.

And he that searcheth the hearts knoweth what is the mind of the Spirit, because he maketh intercession for the saints according to the will of God. Romans 8:27

You'll notice that "the will of" is italicized because it was not in the original Greek but added by translators to make it more readable. Without the italics it reads, "... he maketh intercession for the saints according to God". Thus Christ the intercessor in the heavens generates intercession within your spirit, so that you pray exactly as God would have prayed. Jesus makes intercession through us, so that we now pray beyond our natural limitations, especially the limitation of knowledge. This way, we bypass the challenge Abraham and Moses had due to their limited comprehension of the situation at hand. We are praying on a supernatural plane. This is what praying in tongues is really about. It is like a ladder of elevation above limitations imposed by our humanity (See author's book – The Secret Behind The Secret).

Since we are one spirit with Him (1 Cor. 6:17), the Lord Jesus by the Holy Spirit links up with our human spirit. This way, He prays out His desire as we pray in the spirit. New Testament prayer is cooperation between Jesus in heaven and the believer on earth through the Spirit of God. The Lord Jesus, as Intercessor at the right hand of the Father, has comprehensive insight of events. His insight penetrates into depths that our human brains do not fully grasp and many times know nothing about. He deposits the fragment of His comprehension, which we need to know, into our spirits as supernatural insight, which we then pray out.

Jesus is not actually praying in heaven right now though He is interceding. Jesus does the prayer aspect of His intercession by praying through the recreated spirits of men on the earth. He prays through us supernaturally. He is doing the intercession while we are doing the praying on the basis of His intercession.

We often receive benefits manifested in our lives that we know we have not necessarily believed for or even prayed about. More often than not it is because the Lord Jesus was able to get the substance of the answer through to someone on the earth who supernaturally prayed these into manifestation. The one who prayed is not the source of the goodness, God is. The one who prayed supplied the authority for transferring the goodness in invisible form into the earth, where a man can enjoy it. There are things within the plan of the Lord Jesus for you as the Head of the Church, which you would not experience except as you learn to respond to the promptings of the indwelling Spirit of God.

If the believer who was given a prompting knows what the prompting is about and he knows how to scripturally pray about such, he can pray in his understanding and usher in the intended results of Jesus the intercessor. If however, the believer has a prompting but is unclear as to what the situation is about or how to pray for it effectively, the best response is to pray in tongues. That kind of praying bypasses the limitations of our brain. The believer on the earth does not even need to know what the situation is about. As we yield our authority to Jesus the Intercessor, we are able to usher in the manifestation of supernatural deliverance for others.

Jesus is the head of the body and the body is the fullness of Him. In order for Him to be fully effective on the earth, He engages His body of believers on the earth. There is no variableness in Him, though there is variation in His effectiveness. This is because there is variation in how believers respond to Him when He brings supernatural information by the Holy Spirit to our human spirit. If we do not yield to His prompting to pray and

He is unable to get someone else to yield to Him, He is greatly limited in bringing to pass the manifestation of His will on the earth. As we learn to cooperate with Jesus the Intercessor, believers begin to enjoy His power to save to the uttermost.

People have a will

When praying for others, we want to make sure that we are not violating their will.

Know ye not, that to whom ye yield yourselves servants to obey, his servants ye are to whom ye obey; whether of sin unto death, or of obedience unto righteousness?
Roman 6:16

Authority flows in the direction of our yielding as well as towards what we yield to. No one can rule a man except that man first yields his own will in submission. This is true for saints and sinners alike. Whenever we yield to another, we are effectively causing our authority to flow towards them. When we submit to God, we empower Him in our lives. Our prayers can influence the will of others, who are then ruled by the exercise of their own will.

The type of prayer we have covered in this book is the prayer of faith. It is designed primarily for the one praying it. It is not as effective where the will of another human is concerned. You will get spiritual babies receiving through your faith better than you will get mature Christians to receive through your faith. This is because God wants the older ones to develop their own faith life.

Generally, you would get better results focusing on the things influencing people than you would if you engaged their will headlong.

Repeating your prayers

The implication of the power of choice is that people retain the right to make choices – even wrong choices. Many people abuse this right habitually. By their choices, they continually give the enemy a foothold in their lives. Satan often coincides his attack with when believers sin.. He uses the power of their own choices to hold them bound to him. When we pray for others, there will be delays to the manifestation of answers if they continue to yield to satan's lies. Praying effectively for others would involve repeating our prayers for them. When people commit sin, they are yielding their authority to satan the father of lies. We step in to pray for them scripturally and we obtain answers in its invisible form in the unseen dimension. Their wise choices will hasten the reaping of the full manifestation of answers to our prayers. If however, they persist in making the wrong choices, their choices empower the adversary while invalidating the manifestation of the answer we obtained. When they invalidate our prayers by their choices and habits, we don't give up in despair. We pray again because we understand that the power we released was effective until their own actions released power against themselves, thus cancelling out the effects of our praying. Sometimes people have set their will to change but it takes a while for their actions to catch up with their decision. Their habits have a momentum that causes them to act like they have always acted.

When we pray for others we must not fall for pagan ideas like, "We have five thousand people praying for him, therefore he is sorted". What do numbers have to do with this? We have faith in God's Word and not in the number of people praying.

What do we pray?

We do not ask God to save them. We are praying because salvation is already provided in the death and resurrection of the Lord Jesus. Saving people is no longer a decision that God has to make. He has made that decision once in Christ and now that decision stands forever.

The unbelieving ones are dead in sin and blind in their mind because they do not believe the Word of God. Satan enforces this blindness of heart (2 Cor. 4:3). Therefore, they do not see what God has already done. There is a state of enmity in their mind because of carnal reasoning. So we use our command to break the lordship, which satan enforces through the blindness in their minds and heart. We do not need the permission of the one we are praying for in order to do this. We are exercising our dominion over the spirits that are imposing the condition of blindness. This breaking of blindness suspends the blindness. Once the people exercise their will in wrong decisions again, their action invites satan and triggers the blindness again. This cycle delays manifestation.

While the blindfold over their minds is suspended, they are ready to be reaped as part of God's harvest of precious souls of this earth. In order to be harvested, they need to come in contact with harvesters who reap men for God (Lk. 10:2). So we pray that laborers cross their path to harvest them. God deals with these reapers, who are men that can best influence our loved ones to receive the gift of salvation. We do not respond equally to everyone in life, some people connect with us better than others. These men that could get through with the gospel to our loved ones could themselves delay in responding to God. Worse still, the reapers could yield to religious tradition instead of God's love and power. While the reapers delay, time is going. Through all this, we are praying. Our prayers influence the reapers to go after the lost one with the Word, it also shortens the delay introduced by these reapers.

The saving power of the cross is hidden within the gospel message, which is the power of God unto salvation (Rom. 1:16). The Word of God is the incorruptible seed that is received in order for saving power of God to be released into the life of the lost relative (1 Pet. 1:23). Without the Word, there is no new birth. Again, just because someone is standing in a place where the gospel is being preached does not guarantee that they will receive salvation. Their hearts can tune away from the gospel. So we pray that harvesters present them with the gospel and that they yield to God's Word. While we can exercise dominion over the devil and his blindfolds, we cannot take dominion over the hearts and minds of other human beings whether born again or not.

Our prayers release power, which works in the invisible realm over time. People often maintain their wayward lifestyle, which sows to their flesh, thus they keep storing up corruption for themselves. They are setting up themselves to reap the consequences of sowing to their flesh. We can in the interim remit their sin. We are not focused on how much grief they are causing us to go through; we are concerned about the damage they do to their own soul. When we remit their sins, we temporarily suspend the manifestation of the harvest of the corruption stored up by their lifestyle. We are snatching them out of the fire started by their choices, habits and lifestyle (Jude 23). We cancel out the reaping of their actions, which might have resulted in premature death. We need them alive, so that they can believe the gospel and be transformed by its power. The remitting is in effect until they sow to their flesh again. We then need to cancel out the reaping of those harvests. This cycle keeps repeating itself, until they believe the gospel or time runs out for them. If we act with spiritual intelligence they would be bombarded with opportunity after opportunity to actually hear the good news. The hearing of the good news of the gospel is key.

2

WHO ANSWERED?

There are those who do not know that Jesus has carried all sicknesses and diseases. They believe they are suffering for God's glory through sickness. Others hear their testimony of suffering and they become Christians! Some other people see that and get "sick for God's glory" after praying, "Father God, if it be thy will that through sickness I glorify you, your will be done". That is a dangerous prayer to pray since Peter said that all the sickness that Jesus healed in His ministry was due to satanic oppression (Acts 10:38). Therefore praying as described above is opening the door for satan to wreck havoc on their body. When we pray in ignorance we play into satan's hands. Satan rules through darkness. Satan derives power from our inaccurate praying.

Elijah vs Stephen

There are prayers documented in the Bible, which the Christian should be uncomfortable repeating today because they misrepresent God and stand in opposition to His character as reveled in Christ Jesus. The thinking Christian is honest enough to admit this. Consider this episode from Elijah's life.

Then the king sent unto him a captain of fifty with his fifty. And he went up to him: and, behold, he sat on the top of an hill. And he spake unto him, Thou man of God, the king hath said, Come down.
And Elijah answered and said to the captain of fifty, If I be a man of God, then let fire come down from heaven, and consume thee and thy fifty. And there came down fire from heaven, and consumed him and his fifty.
2 Kings 1:9-10

Contrast this story with Stephen who prayed to God as he was being stoned, "Father do not lay this to their charge". This did not mean that Stephen was more merciful than God. God had found in Stephen what He could not find in Elijah. Stephen responded to provocation with mercy. When provoked, Elijah called down a death-dealing fire from heaven upon his antagonists. It is understandable why at first glance we assume that it was God who answered Elijah's prayer. If we do not rightly divide God's Word, we make Elijah's prayer distort our understanding of what God is really like.

It is worthy of note that only three Old Testament writers mentioned satan. This shows that the Old Testament saints were mostly in the dark and uninformed about his operations. Interestingly every New Testament writer unmasks satan. If you were unaware of satan, you would attribute everything to God. When David sinned by numbering Israel, the people said the "wrath of God" tempted him to do it (2 Sam. 24:1). Centuries later as they received more light from God, they correctly pinned it on satan (1 Chro. 21:1). Even today many do not know how to pinpoint what God did versus what satan did in the Old Testament. Elijah's greatest handicap was that he could not differentiate between God and the "god of this world". Satan as the god of this world tempts men to do evil and brings destruction and death.

James and John tried to reproduce Elijah's death-dealing prayer. Jesus' shocking response to James and John was that Elijah did not know what spirit he was of (Lk. 9:54-55). These disciples were unconsciously yielding to a spirit other than God's Spirit but did not know. Without a doubt, Elijah had a highly developed faith in his God, but since his view of God was distorted it resulted in both bigger mistakes and bigger miracles than other Jews who were not as developed in their faith. Stephen was also a man of power, but he was indwelt by God and was schooled in the love walk.

Elijah's wrath prevented him from differentiating between God's nature and what was likely the influence of another killing and destroying spirit that masquerades as an angel of light. Elijah's wrath opened the door for satan the adversary who Jesus said was the spirit that steals, kills and destroys (John 10:10). If we believe that God was the one who killed those fifty soldiers (2 Kings 1:50) as well as others in the Old Testament, what exactly was satan doing in the Old Testament?

Satan gets his power from men who fail to properly discern the spirit at work. Satan as the prince of the power of the air (Eph. 2:2), tampers with the environment and operates his death-dynamics through agents like sickness, natural disaster, war and famine. In the book of Job, what the men called the fire of God (Job 1:16) was actually satan using fire from the sky to kill and destroy that which was dear to Job (Job 1:12). Job did not rebuke those storms. Jesus however rebuked storms using the same language He used to rebuke evil spirits (Mk. 4:39, Lk. 8:24); thus implying, there was evil intelligence behind these shockwaves in "nature". By His rebukes, Jesus stopped satan from using natural calamities to kill Jesus prematurely. What those men called "the fire of God" was really satan's destructive hand. The righteousness and prayers of the saints enforce the boundaries, which Jesus has placed on satan. When we boldly exercise our authority, we shrink the parameters of satan's boundaries.

Digested as a whole, the New Testament attributes all destructive and homicidal acts to satan as the prince of this world (John 10:10). Satan was willing for the fire to fall from the heavens and bring about the death of many men. That fire travelled on Elijah's wrath. This is why Jesus made that radical statement that James and John (and by extension Elijah) did not know what spirit they were of. Our prayers can open the door for demonic activities, which bring about death and destruction. If we see death and destruction as God answer to prayer, we leave the thief unchallenged, since we think God is at work.

How do you expect God to answer the prayer of a wife who is asking for the death of her husband so she can run away with and marry some other man? God has neither the ability nor willingness to answer such because His nature forbids it. What God's nature forbids, His power will not sustain.

If God were to answer some of what we refer to as prayer, He would become evil. Since God is no respecter of persons (Acts 10:34), He will not answer a prayer just to accommodate your anger while violating the foundation of His own nature and the welfare of others.

Consider this prayer from the Psalms,

Daughter Babylon, doomed to destruction, happy is the one who repays you according to what you have done to us. Happy is the one who seizes your infants and dashes them against the rocks.
Psalm 137:8-9

Did God inspire the psalmist to pray this prayer about dashing the children of enemies against rocks?

More importantly, does God answer this type of prayer? This prayer is at odds with God's nature as revealed in His Son. It is a brutal desire for revenge.

Some people would have us believe that God used to supply the power to destroy these children in the Old Testament and that He does not do so any longer. This would mean that God changed (Mal. 3:6, Num. 23:19, Heb. 13:8). The New Covenant is a change in man and not a change in God! What is God trying to tell us when He answers that kind of prayer? (Notice that question already assumes God is guilty).

A healthier question would be, "Is God involved with that type of prayer at all?"

I believe that God inspired the recording of this prayer as an example of how we must not pray.

Many think that just because such prayers are in the Bible, it must be good. They are preserving a sacred cow. A good conscience compels us to investigate prayers of this slant. The Psalmist anticipates that God rewards those who kill these babies by smashing their heads on the rocks. Fleshly desires of rage are expressed in this prayer. Likely the invading armies had done more despicable things to Jewish babies. Whether these are the babies of Babylon or not, one cannot be a Christian who prays this way! The one who prayed this does not only promote vengeance but finds happiness in killing infants just because they were born to their enemies. This is satanic hatred hiding behind the mask of prayer. Jesus who rebuked his disciples for trying to call down fire would most definitely say of this prayer, "You know not what spirit you are of".

Jesus would have said "Father forgive them for they know not what they do". Concerning our enemies Jesus said we were to be children of God by extending His mercy to our enemies (Lk. 6:36).

The fellow praying is asking God to remember something that the Edomites did in the day that Jerusalem was sacked by an invading force (v7). This could not have been a prayer of David but that of a Jew living in the times of the Babylonian captivity.

This person is praying his emotions. This is deep, dark anger poured out in prayer. There are two broad categories of examples in the Bible (1 Cor. 10:11) and we do well to remember this. There are excellent examples to follow after, since they are consistent with the nature of Christ (Heb. 6:12). There are also clear examples of what we must not follow (Lk. 17:32). You must not assume that just because something is in the Bible, it is OK to repeat it. This is an example of how not to pray.

The contents of this prayer reflect the bruised human heart. It is not the type of prayer Jesus would pray. It does not reflect the divine will. This therefore is a prayer that God cannot answer for it is beyond His ability to propagate that which is unlike Him. God cannot hear and answer a prayer that contradicts His nature. Such praying is beyond the ability of God to answer. This fellow feels he can ask God to do anything to the children of other people, whether those babies were directly responsible for his dark murderous anger or not. People that pray out their emotions, often say things they come to regret. When you go to the house of God, let your words be few and do not offer the sacrifice of fools (Eccl. 5:2). People with damaged hearts end up praying damaging prayers (James 4:2-3).

This makes us affirm that there are unscriptural prayers in the scriptures. We should pattern our prayer life after the Word of

God rightly divided. There are boundaries built into prayer that would prevent me from using God to kill all those who oppose me.

What if a wife prays for the death of her husband, so that she can marry another man and the husband truly dies? Since she prayed to God and her husband is now dead in line with her stated desire, do we insist that God answered her prayers? This looks like an inescapable conclusion until we realise that we can receive answers for any prayer we pray, whether it is God's will or not. It is possible to receive answers that God has not released into our lives.

Don't pray prayers that permits the thief to steal

Sometimes in our zeal to see God reach out to our loved ones, Christians try to make deals with God. We pray saying, "Heavenly Father take from me any possession, position, standing or advantage so that my spouse will accept your salvation?" You can tell whether it is Jehovah such people are making those deals with or some other spirit being by examining what was requested in the light of God's Word. Consider a husband who asks God to put his wife's afflictions on him, so that she can experience freedom from the sickness troubling her. That man is not helping his wife though he intends to. He is inviting tragedy into his own life. By his own will, he has given the enemy permission to attack him with a spirit of infirmity. He has rejected the truth that Jesus bore his wife's sicknesses and diseases (1 Pet. 2:24). He has opened a door through his ill-advised prayer. Asking God to give you the afflictions of someone else is really making deals with the enemy.

Does God permit Satan to wreck that havoc and then sneak in

His salvation? God is not permitting anything. Man is.

Let's observe what is really going on behind the scenes. Satan would camouflage behind this man's prayers of unbelief (He does not believe that the stripes of Jesus healed his wife). The man observes sickness come into his life following his prayer and then concludes that God has answered his prayer. In reality, satan hides behind the man's prayers and wrecks havoc on his health while the man thinks God has acted in response to his prayers. This noble fellow has been ravaged by good intentions. He shares his "testimony" with others who then believe and repeat the same pattern in prayer. Their ignorance causes them to receive satan's wrath which they mistaken for God's goodness. Satan the thief has been welcomed like a friend. The end result is a distorted view of God!

Reflecting the mercy of God

For I perceive that thou art in the gall of bitterness, and in the bond of iniquity. Then answered Simon, and said, Pray ye to the LORD for me, that none of these things which ye have spoken come upon me.
Acts 8:23-24

Apostle Peter had pronounced judgment upon Simon the sorcerer and Simon heard it. Simon's response was that Peter should pray so that none of those things, which Peter had spoken, come to pass. Somehow, Simon the newborn spiritual baby knew that Peter's prayers for Simon could override the earlier judgment. If Simon had died it would be wrong to say God killed him. Man could have shown mercy and not upheld judgment. Ananias and Saphirra's case was not handled this way (See Acts 5).

Ananias and Sapphira gave up the ghost after hearing Peter's words. Peter did not extend to them the mercy that he had received of the Lord when he thrice betrayed Jesus in the early days. Why do we not hear of anyone dropping dead in Jesus ministry? It only looks like God executed Ananias and Sapphira because it happened in a church service. The text does not in any way say that God killed them. Satan is the assassin that destroys the flesh (1 Cor. 5:5). We must remember that the church was still in its infancy. They did not know that the spiritual were to restore brethren who were overtaken in a fault (Gal. 6:1). We have no record that anyone reached out to restore Ananias or Sapphira. No one prayed that their sin not be held against them. This story shows that the saints had a mercy deficiency as much as it shows Ananias and Sapphira had a character and faith deficiency. They did not believe in God's mercy. The condemnation in their heart filled them with too much sorrow and handcuffed the mercy of God. They gave up the will to live. They forsook their own mercy (Jonah 2:8). Physical death filled the void created by condemnation and guilt and rushed in unstopped. Unbelief is spiritual suicide; for it causes us to oppose our own selves (2 Tim. 2:25). Ananias and Sapphira's actions increased Satan's attack surface. Satan participated in their death. That was not the wrath of God!

Satan the thief coincided his attack with their committal of sin. Then due to their misunderstanding of God's true nature, satan's attack was unchallenged. They succumbed to condemnation when by faith they could have resisted the accusation of the destroyer. The result was treated as though it was God's punishment for their wrongdoing.

Ananias and Sapphira heard the words of Peter and they gave up on living. It was easier to die than to live after their public shame. They shut themselves away from the mercy of God. Simon on the other hand heard a stern rebuke by anointed Peter but anticipated that prayer will overturn the outcomes and prevent him from reaping the poison of his own bitterness.

3

UNPLUG FROM THE
MATRIX

The story is told of a young boy who noticed that wherever he saw fire trucks, there were also buildings on fire and what more, wherever the fire trucks parked, he inevitably saw the shell of a burnt down building. His conclusion was that the way to preserve the houses in town was to stop the fire trucks from moving around town, since he reasoned that the fire was a consequence of the movement of the fire trucks. It is true that there is some relationship between fire trucks and houses on fire but the young man had come to the wrong conclusions. The fire preceded the trucks and not the other way round.

The blockbuster film, the Matrix, showcased a world system resulting from a coup by machines that use humans as "batteries" to power their system. These machines projected images that enslaved the people with false simulations that immersed the people in delusion. Neo, who was the main actor, swallowed a pill that caused him to wake up to who he really was. He then became aware that the people were connected to a system that put them in a continuous dream state!

Replace those machines with religion and the simulations with our traditions and a picture emerges. Religion (ab)uses human power to sustain its structures while blinding men to the realities of who God really is. As a consequence, believers do not know who they really are. Man first plugged into the matrix of religion and satan's simulations when he ate of the tree of the knowledge of good and evil in the Garden.

Eating from the tree of life

Whereby are given unto us exceeding great and precious promises: that by these ye might be partakers of the divine nature, having escaped the corruption that is in the world through lust.
2 Peter 1:4

You are what you eat. We are called to feast on God, to feed fully on His nature for nutrition. The spirit of man is now one with God. Understanding union with Christ is difficult for most people because they never quite understood union with sin. They thought that they were not really bad without Christ but that they have just made a decision that takes them to heaven.

What the tree of life was in the Garden of Eden, the divine nature is to the new creation man. Adam had the tree of life in the midst of the Garden of Eden, but he did not eat of it. It is one thing to possess the tree of life but having access to the tree does not equate to partaking of it. It is God's plan that you and I as believers eat off the tree of life continually. Eating off the tree of life means living by the faith of Christ, which He supplies within as a gift. The whole story about the tree of life and the tree of the knowledge of good and evil contains lessons for us today. Rather than eating off the tree of life, the majority of the Church eat off the tree of the knowledge of good and evil. The tree of the knowledge of good and evil is soulish, for it is knowledge derived apart from God. Eating off the tree of the knowledge of good and evil brought the curse upon Adam and today it represents coming under the curse by attempting to live through the works of the Law (Gal. 3:10).

Eating off the tree of the knowledge of good and evil is the elevation of the soul above the spirit and the crowning of intellect as god. Those that eat off the tree of life judge all things by the spirit of life within while the ones who eat off the tree of the knowledge of good and evil discern all things through their appearance via the senses. People who live by the senses while shunning the faith walk barricade themselves out of their own spirits where the life of God is.

In the New Covenant, we partake of God's divine nature within as we eat of the precious bread of the Word and drink of His Spirit. This divine nature is the covenant that God has with the Lord Jesus. Feasting on the Word is the equivalent of the eating of the covenant meal. All the eating and feasting is designed to bring us to that place where we believe that the life within us is able for all situations. This is the way, truth and life that Jesus talked about. The New Covenant is not an event but a union of spirits; our spirit joined with God's Spirit (1 Cor. 6:17). We are not apart from Him but are in fact one spirit with Him. By His divine nature within us we have become one with God forever. He is not in the heavens trying to give something to us. He is reaching out from within us. He is flowing out of us to meet any need.

Within the matrix of religion, you have those who seek to be controlled by others as well as those who live to control others.

The desire to be controlled by others is also a manifestation of eating off the wrong tree. It is God's plan that rather than allowing others control us or perhaps succumbing to the temptation to control others, we should keep eating off the tree of life and learn to flow from authority.

This story of the prodigal son (See Lk. 15:18-32) illustrates how religion blinds people with illusions that prevent them from enjoying their inheritance. If on his return that younger brother had first met the older brother, that younger man would never have made it home.

Religion is a mass-production factory that keeps producing more of the elder-brother type. Worldliness produces the younger brother type. That father had lost two sons, the younger to the world and the older to religion. Still he always wanted to celebrate his sons.

God is in party mood for His dead son is alive again, but the religious heart of the elder brother turns God's party into a time of sadness. The religious brother is sad and he feels that everyone else must be sad with him. Man who is full of death hinders God who is life from unveiling His fullness. The Father has no accusations while the elder son cannot stop accusing and blaming. Accusation is the mother tongue of fallen man. Religion controls people through condemnation. It is as we renew our mind with God's Word that we speak the mother tongue of our spirit, which is acceptance with, as well as belonging in the family of God.

Can you pick the pain in this father's voice? There are things that he has guessed all the while about this elder son of his that have now been confirmed by his outburst. This elder son lamented, "But I have waited for years without having that calf, why then did you give it to my younger brother?" It is true that the elder brother had waited indefinitely but his father confirms to him that he could have had that calf at any time of his choosing.

Was the younger son more receptive and more aware of the celebration spirit of the father than the elder brother was? What shock this must have been to that elder brother. He is the son that never left home but he was not there for his father nor could he share in his father's joy. His emotional life was plugged into another stream. He accused both his Father and His Father's younger son. He is the voice of the Accuser. Satan's ability to accuse is derived from men who are willing to peddle accusations.

All that God has is yours

The religious elder brother did not say, "my brother". He said, "your son". That elder son would have gone to bed that night thinking, "You mean I could have had the calf at any time?" The only reason why he never killed that calf was because he assumed that it was up to his Father to decide when the calf was killed. He thought that his father determined when the calf could be taken. His father must have wondered why his elder son had chosen to forego the enjoyment of what was rightfully his by relationship. The elder son had waited for long only because he was the type that believes that the act of waiting long has spiritual merit and is a basis on which God takes pity. There are Christians, sons of the Father God, who are very much like this older son. They believe God quite all right but their faith is in waiting for long before enjoying the Father's provision. They experience the delay they brought on themselves while assuming that "delay" was the Father's modus operandi.

The father had been willing for a long time for his elder son to take that calf. The son did not understand his father and his ignorance stopped him from taking the calf. He was waiting to earn enough brownie points with his father, so that the father would consider him worthy of having the fattened calf. He was plugged into the matrix of religion feeding a delusion of his own creation, all the while thinking that his father was training him in patience. Biblical patience follows faith (James 1:3). It can only be exercised when we believe what God believes about a situation. It is people that have released their faith that require patience. Unbelief does not call upon patience.

Religion and unbelief bear false witness against God's nature. There is a well-known but little-understood commandment that reads, "Thou shall not bear false witness". A false witness is that which is contrary to the truth of who we are because of who God is. Don't tell a lie or live a lie against the nature of God within you. Whatever the Word says about us is truth and all else are appearances and products of the senses in a fallen world.
The elder son lived in a matrix where he thought the father was withholding the calf from him. That was his tradition - and his reality but he was wrong. The adversary had stolen his father's words from his heart so that he never really understood his own father. A soul devoid of the knowledge of God's Word keeps us plugged into the dangerous matrix of religion. The matrix of religion causes us to hear lofty things about God while remaining delusional about what it means. This forces our prayer life into "waiting for God to kill the fatted calf" rather than acknowledging and taking. Meditation on the Word switches you out of the matrix! Swallow God's love medicine and wake out of the slumber of religion and delusion!

God gives

He that spared not his own Son, but delivered him up for us all, how shall
he not with him also freely give us all things?
Romans. 8:32

There is a principle in Genesis, spoken to Noah after the flood and it is a principle that governs the earth. It is the powerful principle of sowing and reaping (Genesis 8:22). It is a law and it works in the earth realm as long as the earth remains. It is not the principle that governs heaven or the universe and it is not a spiritual law. It is a valid way of operating. It is not to be confused with God's preferred method of relating to us. As a Father, it is the Father's good pleasure to give you the kingdom (Luke 12:32). This is operating by the Father's giving versus operating by the reaping of that which we have sowed. How does a God who is a giver communicate to carnal man who wants to earn?

In prayer, we have the opportunity to obtain answers because we have "sowed" for them. We can also obtain answers because the Father has given them to us freely. This higher law, which is a spiritual law, states that because God did not spare His son but delivered him up for us all, He freely and richly gives us all things (Rom. 8:32). Based on this principle, we approach the Father because He is a giver. It takes a while to switch out of the lower law, which is tied to the earth and to switch to the higher law, which is tied to the Fatherhood of God. The Father has given us His son whether we believe it or not. It is a spiritual fact. The natural man struggles to believe this because he is not alive to spiritual facts. Before you start praying learn to praise Him for what He says is already yours. God loves to feast and throw a party celebrating you. Don't wait for him to kill the fatted calf. It is yours for the asking and taking. God is a lavish giver. God is in party mood. Feast with him.

4

CONSIDER HIS MIRACLES

And he went up unto them into the ship; and the wind ceased: and they were sore amazed in themselves beyond measure, and wondered. For they considered not the miracle of the loaves: for their heart was hardened.
Mark 6:51-52

There was evil intelligence behind the storm, an unseen hand, which wanted these men dead. Jesus was aware of this evil intelligence though the disciples were clueless that their hard heart was the window through which that hand was gaining influence. A hard heart is neither good nor bad. It is what your heart is hard towards that is key. Their hearts were hard towards God's power. That is not cool! You want your heart hardened against doubt and confusion. These disciples loved Jesus. They were religious and zealous but were struggling for dear life until Jesus walked into their boat. Jesus was walking on the same water that was about to kill those disciples.

This is not a case of God abandoning the disciples to die because they were surplus to requirement while feeling a need to protect Jesus by all means. God was not the variable, hardness of heart was. Their hearts were hardened because "they considered not the miracle of the loaves". Thus the principle is that whatever you refuse to consider, you become hardened towards. By the same principle, your heart softens towards whatever you pay attention to.

A hard heart handcuffs the mercy of God and bows the knees to premature death. These men were shocked when they saw Jesus trampling upon the very thing that was about to usher them into the grave. Jesus remembered the feeding of the five thousand. This fed His miracle consciousness. The disciples' shock is proof they did not have a miracle consciousness. People with a hard heart see death as the only outcome of a storm. A hard heart is the logic that fails to anticipate the supernatural. We stand in awe of God's power but we are never shocked to see it at work. We should be tender hearted towards God's power while we remain hard hearted towards death, lack and failure.

> *And he charged them, saying, Take heed, beware of the leaven of the Pharisees, and of the leaven of Herod. And they reasoned among themselves, saying, It is because we have no bread. And when Jesus knew it, he saith unto them, Why reason ye, because ye have no bread? perceive ye not yet, neither understand? have ye your heart yet hardened? Having eyes, see ye not? and having ears, hear ye not? and do ye not remember? When I brake the five loaves among five thousand, how many baskets full of fragments took ye up? They say unto him, Twelve. And when the seven among four thousand, how many baskets full of fragments took ye up? And they said, Seven. And he said unto them, How is it that ye do not understand?*
> *Mark 8:15-21*

Their spiritual perception was dull because their spiritual senses were undeveloped. They could not see or sense the supernatural. The power of God was present but a hard heart blinded them from seeing it. The answer was present as well as the challenge but they only acknowledged the challenge. The rest of our Christian journey is dependent on our understanding what happened with the miracle of loaves. A visit to God's bakery is important for your spiritual health.

Jesus said that their journey was intensely difficult because the disciples did not remember the important things. They reasoned in unbelief from a sense of what they did not have on them. They were untrained in the type of reasoning that engages miraculous supply. Too many believers are trying to pray from a heart that is hardened against God's miracle supply. They believe in the supernatural but they reason from lack. The chief characteristic of this type of Christians is that when they pray, they are asking because "they have not".

They panicked because they reasoned that they only had one loaf! Unbelief dulled them to the resident power of God that was available in Jesus. Jesus taught them to reason from the possibilities locked within God's power. He was telling them that the same power that used 5 loaves to feed 5,000 men with twelve baskets of extras left at the end was in that boat. They did not need more power and God did not need more time in the gym. Unbelief had shut their creative vision. If they had been up for it they could have had a party in the midst of that storm for there was abundance of power and one loaf of bread.

And they say unto him, We have here but five loaves, and two fishes. He said, Bring them hither to me. And he commanded the multitude to sit down on the grass, and took the five loaves, and the two fishes, and looking up to heaven, he blessed, and brake, and gave the loaves to his disciples, and the disciples to the multitude. And they did all eat, and were filled:

and they took up of the fragments that remained twelve baskets full.
Matthew 14:17-20

Jesus started with a sense of availability. He wanted to know what was available. We often start with what we don't have.

He blessed the five loaves. Greek scholars tell us that the word "bless" means to speak well of or to praise. Jesus released the power of abundance by staying full of praise to God for what He already held in His hands. You can measure the hardness of your heart by watching how often you praise. People that reason from lack are too fretful to acknowledge what is already theirs in Christ. They therefore fail to see what is already in their possession. They think that they do not have. They are convinced that they have nothing. They are asking for the wrong reasons. God's power of multiplication works best when we are thankful for what He says is ours in Christ already. Some folks are unable to praise God for the friends that they have but are forever tense talking to God about the friend of their dreams. The one they do not have. They fail to bless God. Praise cures our hearts of hardness. As you praise God for the friends that you have, you release yourself to experience the power that multiplies true friends.

5

GOD'S HOLINESS RESCUES US

Many are robbed of developing a robust prayer life because of a faulty understanding of the holiness of God. They run away from Him because they believe that His holiness would kill them.

As for our redeemer, the LORD of hosts is his name, the Holy One of Israel.
Isaiah 47:4

Our Redeemer is the Holy One

I used to think that the holiness of God demanded that He punishes us for our faults while His love sort of placated Him. I believed that my experiences depended on whether God was in a love mood or a holiness mood. If our sins can separate

God from us, then we are hopelessly lost and stuck forever in our misery. Many think that the holiness of God is something to run away from whenever they make a mistake. This is due to an unfortunate understanding of the holiness of God. In truth, God redeemed us because He is the Holy One. His holiness is the very reason why He reaches out to redeem us thus separating us from our sins. His holiness separates us to himself.

God is not a holy God in that He separates Himself from sinners but in that He separates us from our sins. His holiness separates us from these mucky, dark, weird things that we join ourselves to spiritually. His holiness propels Him to reach out to us and overcome our sins as our Redeemer.

Jesus is the greatest demonstration of God's holiness. No man was a Christian before Jesus died and rose from the dead; therefore all that He met with were sinners. We don't find Him staying away from people when He was on earth. His incarnation is proof that genuine holiness is social and deeply relational. Jesus destroys our neat assumptions that sin separates God from us. The Pharisees could see that Jesus was the friend of sinners. He failed their holiness test. Jesus makes it impossible for us to hold on to the idea that sin separates God from us. God has personally corrected our ideas of His holiness by sending Jesus. He was manifested to separate us from sins as well as the nature of sin. Jesus is the best "Bible" translation. He translates God. He translates the beauty of holiness.

And you, that were sometime alienated and enemies in your mind by
wicked works, yet now hath he reconciled
Colossians 1:21

It is plain to see that there is alienation between man and God but it is not because God is holy. The alienation between man and God is in the mind of man and is one-sided. Man became God's enemy and banished God by elevating the testimony of his own senses above the testimony of divine revelation. Sin corrupted the mind and our lives through wicked works. When a man receives eternal life, his mind is largely unchanged. Therefore, he still fights battles having to do with acceptance with God. This is because the mind until renewed by God's Word actively enforces alienation. The human mind alienates God. Satan seizes upon this to deceive man that it is actually God that has banished man from His presence! That kind of thinking clouds even our reading of God's Word because sin consciousness veils the mind from the light of God's Word. Until a Christian deliberately believes in God's love, he continues to experience his own self-imposed alienation even though God fully accepted him in Christ Jesus. Redemption is the rescue of our thoughts from Satan-inspired mistrust of God.

Prayer is letting your communion with God move your eyes to see His goodness. Prayer is seeing so much in the face of Christ that the make-belief of this earth's sphere and the false simulations of religion no longer hypnotize you. Prayer is coming under the hypnosis of God's love.

Religious traditions say that God's holiness demands that He severely punish sins.

God inspires Isaiah to say:

For thus saith the high and lofty One that inhabiteth eternity, whose name is Holy; I dwell in the high and holy place, with him also that is of a contrite and humble spirit, to revive the spirit of the humble, and to revive the heart of the contrite ones.
Isaiah 57:15

The Bible teaches that God's holiness demands that He revives (or gives life to) man.

Behold, the LORD's hand is not shortened, that it cannot save; neither his ear heavy, that it cannot hear: But your iniquities have separated between you and your God, and your sins have hid his face from you, that he will not hear.
Isaiah 59:1-2

This passage in Isaiah is one of the first clear explanations of the why of that separation that exists between man and God.

It does not say that sin separates God from us. In the early days, I read that verse to say that sin separates God from us. I believed that to be the case even though that was not quite what was written! It is self-evident that sin does not have the power to do that to God. What it does say is that sin separated us from God. This enmity was in our minds. This means that it is our consciousness of sin that corners us into a state of alienation from God. This is a one-sided alienation enforced by our unbelief. God does not alienate Himself from us.

Today, many Christians reason in ways that alienate them from God. God does not want us to major on the problem of sin but on His omnipotent love, which supplies the grace of God. As we become strong in the grace of God, we find ability within that grace to rise above the mess of carnality. The grace of God resets our minds and ends the enmity so that we can enjoy the holiness of God.

To wit, that God was in Christ, reconciling the world unto himself, not imputing their trespasses unto them; and hath committed unto us the Word of reconciliation.
2 Corinthians. 5:19

We were God's enemies but He was not ours. God had no hostility in His own heart to deal with. Sin changed us but God did not change. Therefore the blood of Christ did not appease

God. The blood of Christ did not reconcile God but man. Man was always the one needing reconciliation. God used the Cross of Christ to dismantle our hostility towards Him and not God's hostility towards us. God did this through the blood of Christ. Let the mercy of God displayed in Christ change your attitude towards God's holiness and free you to see what God has already done about your sins. Changing your mind about the desirableness of sin is a mark of maturity. There is nothing desirable about sin. You should not allow sin separate you from God any longer. The devil will team up with religion to deceive your mind into allowing your slips, errors, mistakes and faults do this to you. You need to remember that the Father God, through the blood of Jesus has forgiven you of all your sins. No matter the accusation of satan, do not let go of your understanding of God's holiness or your precious fellowship with the Father. In the final analysis, Christianity is not about sin; it's about fellowship with God. Though God's holiness has rescued us and dealt with all sins for all time, people still reject His grace and do not believe in His accomplishments. Man believes his own works more than the works of Christ. The absence or presence of sins has never been the issue. The issue is one of unbelief and the abuse of the will. Unbelief is delusional because while people are going out of their way to avoid God, they remain convinced that it is God avoiding them!

Our hearts condemn us

For if our heart condemn us, God is greater than our heart, and knoweth all things. Beloved, if our heart condemn us not, then have we confidence toward God.
1 John 3:20-21

God did not leave it up to us to initiate our fellowship with Him, it is the handiwork of God (1 Cor. 1:9). Our fellowship with God is a calling that God never withdraws. We might fail to embrace it or be dulled through sin into disbelieving it but nevertheless the fellowship stands sure. Satan needs you to believe the lie that he can kill your fellowship with God. He cannot. He accuses your heart so you do this deadly job yourself as unbelief causes you to agree with the accusations arising in your heart. If you believe that your fellowship with God is gone because you sinned, your unbelief enforces alienation between you and God.

We are not as quick to forgive our own selves as God is quick to forgive us. We think that God is holding against us the very things that we are holding against ourselves. This robs us of confidence. When our heart accuses that our fellowship with God is gone, we are to remember that the fellowship still exists for Jesus has not changed His mind. We are still the brothers of the Lord and God remains our Father. I must stop committing the sin of allowing my heart operate as the final authority in the matter instead of allowing the Word. Rather than allowing your heart such liberties, pray out loud the Word of reconciliation, which unfolds to you the redemption that we have in Christ. This prayer will bring assurance to your heart through the Word.

Prayer takes on its intended meaning when you no longer think that sin is bigger than God. You admit God has done something about sin because He is bigger than sin. Now you are to move on by cooperating with His desires within you, so that His desires and yours are one and the same. This is fellowship.

Be consumed by God's desire

For God is working in you, giving you the desire and the power to do what pleases him.
Philippians 2:13 (NLT)

God's powerful desire is always stirred up within us; we just need to learn to cooperate with that desire and allow it animate our whole being. God is always at work within us seeking that we cooperate with Him to co-author peace in our world. This is His good pleasure. God is not limited by anything in the whole universe except by His own self and His nature. God's nature does not override another, therefore He is not controlling everyone nor does He ride roughshod over all. Our fleshly definition of God allows for such. If we were God, in all likelihood we would fix things such that we got exactly what we wanted and ensured that only what we wanted could ever happen. This quality is not in God at all. God's desire is that we desire together with Him. He waits in the hope that this becomes our consuming desire. God desires that we work together with Him to bring these desires into being. We find our delight in the desires of God. This is the will of God, which works in us as new creation men.

I will

And there came a leper to him, beseeching him, and kneeling down to him, and saying unto him, If thou wilt, thou canst make me clean. And Jesus, moved with compassion, put forth his hand, and touched him, and saith unto him, I will; be thou clean. And as soon as he had spoken, immediately the leprosy departed from him, and he was cleansed.
Mark 1:40-42

Christianese has its strange phraseology. In our everyday speech we don't say, "I will come visit you tomorrow because it is your will for me to do so". We simply don't speak this way at all. In the society in which the King James Version was translated, they spoke this way but meant something altogether different than our usage today. The Greek word often translated, as "will" also means that which we delight in, desire or take pleasure in. Today, the Word "will" carries the idea of that which is inevitable, resolute, as well as the ability of conscious choice and intention. This misses the mark altogether and causes us to dread the will of God, as we do not know that this is divine opportunity to be caught up in God's higher desires and delights.

Greek scholars tell us that there was another Greek word Jesus could have used when He said, "I will" (it is Strong's number 2309 versus 1014). That word "2309" means a delighting in as disposition of nature. Jesus was not just saying, "I am making a choice for this instant therefore I will do it for you this time". We read that idea into the statement in the English language, but in the Greek, He is laying down a marker in eternity and saying this is who I am. He was not making a choice at that instant, rather He was saying "I am always willing and forever willing because within my nature is a restless intensity of desire. I always act on my nature which is a delivering nature". Jesus was showing that His willingness was not a consequence of the Leper's request but a disposition of His nature. He will always deliver on this.

This Leper basically says, "If you will, you can". Religion is big on God's ability but uncertain as to His will. This state of affairs grieves any father. God is willing and able. Due to what we know about God's intensity of desire to deliver, if we find ourselves at crossroads tempted to question His willingness or His ability (not that we should question any of the two), we should question His ability and not His willingness. God can be trusted to do all that He can. It would thrill me if my son tells me "Dad I know you'd help me if you could" rather than "I know you can help but for some reason you are not willing to".

Build your life on the rock

Whosoever cometh to me, and heareth my sayings, and doeth them, I will shew you to whom he is like: He is like a man which built an house, and

digged deep, and laid the foundation on a rock: and when the flood arose, the stream beat vehemently upon that house, and could not shake it: for it was founded upon a rock. But he that heareth, and doeth not, is like a man that without a foundation built an house upon the earth; against which the stream did beat vehemently, and immediately it fell; and the ruin of that house was great.
Luke 6:47-49

It was the same wind, rain, and flood that beat on both houses, but their outcomes were different. Jesus does not teach that the determinant was God's will that one stand while the other falls. The same rock was available to both to build their foundation on, but only one placed a premium on doing what he heard Jesus say. Stability is God's choice. God has outlawed uncertainty by giving us His word; all else is permitted by us.

A house built on the rock does not necessarily mean a life built on Christ. Every Christian is built on Christ otherwise he is not a Christian to start with. We are to build our lives on the rock of hearing the Lord Jesus with our heart and doing what we hear Him say to us in His word as well as within our spirit. Build your prayer life on God's Word.

The secret of stability is in God's Word. You release that stabilizing power by acting on the Word. Your decision to choose God's choice and act on it causes you to stand no matter what.

He gave because He loved

For God so loved the world, that he gave his only begotten Son, that whosoever believeth in him should not perish, but have everlasting life.
John 3:16

God did not give Jesus to the world because He had the power to do so. God gave because He loved. His love is the explanation of His power. His love is the reason for His power. Though God is all-powerful, He does not save because He has the power to do so. He saves because of His love nature. We are more prone to appeal to God's power than to His love. However whatever God does, He does because He loves. In the same vein, God does not answer our prayers because He is the all-powerful and almighty one (though He is all that and more). He answers because of what the Lord Jesus has accomplished. In Him all the promises of God are yes and Amen (2 Cor. 1:20). God's nature is love and He cannot be anything other than love. Approach Him because He loves your approach. You are not beyond the reach of God's love.

6

COVENANT CONSCIOUS

Blessed be the God and Father of our Lord Jesus Christ, who hath blessed us with all spiritual blessings in heavenly places in Christ:
Ephesians 1:3

In order to appreciate the force of those words we must be able to distinguish between what we moderns refer to as contracts and what the ancient societies refer to as covenant. Contracts have two parties who remain distinct and separate while Covenants unify and produce a new whole. Covenants free us and impart privileges while contracts burden us with duties while binding us. People look for ways to break contracts without suffering penalties whereas the parties in a covenant don't want to get out of it. While contracts appeal to our intellect, covenants penetrate beyond the mind and reach into our guts and our hearts. Covenants and contracts are therefore not equivalent terms. Covenants means next to nothing to our supposedly sophisticated postmodern world.

Parties in a blood covenant form a brotherhood. Scholars tell us that the expression "Blood is thicker than water" is better rendered "Blood is thicker than milk". It is a term used by ancient societies who understood the sacredness of the blood covenant. The term means that a brotherhood which is derived via a blood covenant is stronger than one derived through being born of the same mother. The Bible majors on covenants. Abraham had a covenant with God.

And he believed in the Lord; and he counted it to him for righteousness. And it came to pass, that, when the sun went down, and it was dark, behold a smoking furnace, and a burning lamp that passed between those pieces. In the same day the Lord made a covenant with Abram, saying, Unto thy seed have I given this land, from the river of Egypt unto the great river, the river Euphrates:
Genesis 15:6,17,18

Notice that God cut a covenant by saying, "Unto thy seed ...". Men are significantly affected by blood while God is affected by His own Word. Just as men find covenants unbreakable, God treats His Word as His unbreakable covenant.

God walked through the blood of those animals to prove to Abraham that He was willing to be Abraham's covenant partner. As was the custom then, Abraham as the other covenant partner should also have walked through the blood. God mercifully took a different route by putting Abraham to sleep instead of demanding that Abraham fulfill his part. While Abraham slept, God showed him the future. God then took Abraham's place and walked through the blood a second time. God was proving to Abraham how committed He was to the performance of His Word to Abraham. Abraham's part was to believe and enjoy the benefits while God carried all the risks! Abraham was familiar with the idea of two men committing themselves to each other in the knowledge that violation of the terms carried the death penalty. He had never seen anything like deity giving a man iron clad guarantees. The aim of this blood covenant is to assure Abraham's heart of the certainty and integrity of God's Word. God was willing to go that far.

But now hath he obtained a more excellent ministry, by how much also he is the mediator of a better covenant, which was established upon better promises.
Hebrews 8:6

When the writer of Hebrews speaks of a better covenant, he is comparing the New Covenant with another covenant, a national covenant, entered into between God and Abraham's children after they were released from captivity in Egypt. They promised to keep their part of the Covenant! They forgot that even Abraham made no such promises to God! That other covenant was between men and God. God found fault with it. It did not work. In the New Covenant, God is not trying to prove that another covenant between God and each of us will work. We must not treat the New Covenant as though it is an upgrade of the Old Covenant with new characters. The New Covenant is not between God and you. The New is not like the Old (Heb. 8:9). It is between God and the Son of Man, the Lord Jesus. As the Mediator, Jesus represented man fully as the son of Man, which was His preferred term for Himself. He also represented God as the Son of God. In Him, God and man meet. Jesus was also the sacrifice of the covenant.

This New Covenant has more in common with the covenant that God cut with Abraham when he put Abraham to sleep than the National covenant that God cut with Israel in the wilderness. This New Covenant is personal. The blood covenant is between the Lord Jesus and the Father God. Jesus as the Son of God represented God's side of the covenant and as the Son of Man, He represented man's side. When one breaks a blood covenant, he is inviting his own death. God and the Lord Jesus are obliged to put the other to death if either breaks the covenant. They are not looking to put us to death. Our part is to believe. The New Birth makes you a beneficiary of the Covenant between God and Jesus.

What exists between God the Father and the Lord Jesus Christ is an unbreakable covenant. The two parties in this covenant never change and cannot lie. When you pray, God is not looking for a reason to deny the request. He knows you qualify because you are "In Christ". Jesus qualifies you. God looks at His nature within you. This is your qualification. This is why you can expect answers.

By a new and living way

Having therefore, brethren, boldness to enter into the holiest by the blood of Jesus, By a new and living way, which he hath consecrated for us, through the veil, that is to say, his flesh;
Hebrews 10:19-20

That term "a new and living way" is a reference to the recreated human spirit; for the New Covenant is impossible without the recreation of the human spirit. This means the nature of God within our reborn spirits. The New Covenant is God writing His nature on our hearts. The New Covenant is that consciousness of oneness with God through oneness with Christ because we are possessors of the same nature as God (John 17:20).

As believers, we are to approach boldly in prayer based on the blood of another. The boldness of our approach is the precious blood of Jesus. Our boldness rests on the faith of Jesus. We believe in His unbending faithfulness to the Father. Our boldness is not based on our faithfulness. This New Covenant is a person. Jesus is the New Covenant (Heb. 10:16-23). His blood and ours have become one (1 Cor. 6:17). We are one spirit with Him. We are what He is. We no longer view God as "another".

In this regard, His blood means that I believe that I will receive my answers through the qualification of Jesus instead of relying on the rightness or loudness of my voice, rites or rituals. He has given us the use of His name. The name represents the price that He paid as well as the depth of His anguish and triumph just so that you can have your answers in prayer.

7

RIGHT & WRONG PRAYING

The idolatry of much speaking

But when ye pray, use not vain repetitions, as the heathen do: for they think that they shall be heard for their much speaking.
Matthew 6:7

Jesus is David's smooth rock shattering the head of our Goliath of religious thinking and unbelief as He discusses prayer. According to Jesus, one can be quoting the Bible and yet praying like a pagan. We would readily associate paganism with dancing weirdly to demonic drumbeats and blood sacrifices. We rightly distance ourselves from such practices. Jesus teaches that adopting vain repetition in prayer is pagan practice too. It is not just what you quote or how dogmatic you are about it. Why we think we will be heard (or not heard) is as important as what we say in prayer. All we say in prayer becomes meaningless pagan repetition if we think that we will be heard for our much speaking. Some people are assured of answers to prayer because ten thousand saints are praying for them. They are relying on much speaking. Your philosophy in prayer is the beginning of praying itself. Let the Word of God build into you God's philosophy concerning prayer.

God does not go around with a stopwatch in His hand measuring how long we spend in prayer in order to determine when He will answer. If you think that God will hear you because you have spent a long time saying a lot to Him in prayer, that kind of thinking is pagan. A man that thinks that way does not require the devil to hinder him. He is already good at opposing his own self. Long prayers are not more effective than short prayers. How much would be left of our prayer if we stripped away all repetition?

Some people say the "Our Father who art in heaven" prayer at the end of every service as a way of signaling that the service has come to a close. They are not necessarily praying per se, just serving notice to everyone present that it is time to go home. Anyone listening might be fooled into thinking that they are addressing God but in reality they are performing the last rites to bring the service to an end. At best they are speaking to one another. Praying in tongues extensively is a form of spiritual communion and a means to release tremendous power for later use.

Prayer is taught

And it came to pass, that, as he was praying in a certain place, when he ceased, one of his disciples said unto him, Lord, teach us to pray, as John also taught his disciples.
Luke 11:1

The disciples of Jesus and the disciples of John were devout Jews who like the typical devout Jew prayed five times a day towards Jerusalem. Praying five times a day did not imply that they knew how to pray. It is possible to routinely go through the motions of prayer multiple times daily and still not be praying! John noticed their deficiency, and then taught his disciples about prayer. People don't pray intelligently by accident. Once the disciples of Jesus observed Jesus pray they quickly came to the conclusion that in spite of their rich religious pedigree they were deficient in their execution of prayer. A lot of what Jesus taught concerning prayer upstages our fanciful theologies, if we really pay attention to them.

As you have received Christ

As ye have therefore received Christ Jesus the Lord, so walk ye in him: Rooted and built up in him, and stablished in the faith, as ye have been taught, abounding therein with thanksgiving.
Colossians 2:6,7

Take out time to understand the basics of salvation because that is the basis of everything else. The rest of your Christian life is a walk to become established in the marvelous things that already happened in your spirit man the moment that you received salvation. It is as you become established in these that the riches flow out of your inner life through thanksgiving to God. People who function by the faith of Christ tend to be people who praise God a lot.

Pay close attention to how Paul said you got born again, "As you have received Christ Jesus the Lord …"

When describing the New Birth, we often say that we gave our lives to Jesus. The truth is that we were dead in sins therefore, had no life to give to ourselves less so to another person. We did not give our life to Jesus. We received Him as our life. Since we did not offer the Lord our fasting, good manners and exemplary life as payment for eternal life, we cannot use the same things as bargaining material in order to get God to give us things. We did not earn salvation by works; therefore, we cannot obtain answered prayers by works. The grace that brought us salvation is also the foundation for answered prayers.

If you do not stay full of praise, faith will not be in full flow. Thanksgiving establishes you in faith and causes faith to become more accessible for our use. The more you practice a lifestyle of thanksgiving, the more your faith abounds until it brings full manifestation (Col. 2:7). Through receiving satan's doubts you hinder yourself from enjoying the riches that are yours in Christ. Mature Christians do not spend all their time praying without letting prayer give way to praise. Prayer without praise is frustration. Never pray so much that you forget the praise cure. Praise will cure you of the limiting mindset of the world. There are mindsets in prayer that cause us not to reason like God. While the correct mindset to adopt in prayer might not be immediately obvious, the mindset that caused us to receive salvation is well known. Start with the known in order to master the unknown.

The day you got born again was not the day God saved you, it was the day you received him. The gift had always been available but you were not always aware of the fact, therefore, you could not receive. The key concept of your salvation was that you learnt to receive by believing. Since you are to walk in Christ the same way you received Him, it means that all that you need for the rest of your life is already provided in gift form by God's grace. You just might not be able to receive the provision and just as with salvation, the challenge is not on God's side but on man's side.

What can you do to get yourself to a place where God hears you?

Do you have to be good enough?

Jesus deserves your answered prayers just as He deserves your salvation.

You cannot pray and fast your way into God answering your prayer any more than praying and fasting your way for God to save you.

Answers to prayer are not based on works. Jesus is our foundation for answered prayers. I have a right to answered prayers because Jesus deserves it. This is basically what it means to pray in His name. We don't pray in our name because it is not about what we did but what He did. Since Jesus bore what you were, He deserves that your prayers be answered. It is arrogance to anticipate answers to prayer because you did everything right.

God already sent Jesus

The gospel of salvation requires you to believe that Jesus already died for your sins and that God has already raised Him up for your justification without your asking Him to (Rom. 10:9).

The gospel of salvation is not the good forecast. That gospel does not look to the future but to the past; therefore, it is properly called good news. It reports the already-accomplished salvation of God. All that it majors on derive from what God has already accomplished and provided in Christ Jesus. The premise of the born again experience therefore, is that God has already accomplished my salvation. I am not making Him save me but believing instead that He already has saved and forgiven me. All that I am doing is receiving this salvation and forgiveness through the blood, so that I experience salvation in my spirit man. In prayer you are not trying to get God to do something for you that He has not already done in Christ. You are acknowledging what He has done and releasing its effects into your life through prayer. To believe otherwise is really to believe against the revealed Word of God.

The sting of death is sin; and the strength of sin is the law. But thanks be to God, which giveth us the victory through our Lord Jesus Christ.
1 Corinthians 15:56-57

When the Law was given in Exodus 19 it wasn't a reflection of God's heart toward man. God did not want the Law; He wanted a relationship where every Jew was a priest (Ex. 19:6). The people rejected God's offer saying, "Whatever He tells us to do we will do" so God obliged them with the Law (Deut. 5:27). It was man who wanted the Law.

We do not expect God to say of His own Law that the strength of sin is the Law! This means that the Law did not empower us against sin; instead it empowered the expression of sin! The shocking truth is that the Law strengthens the expression of that which it forbids. We expect a holy Law would only stir holiness but that is not the case. The Law strengthens sin and not righteousness. Therefore, we don't get people praying by preaching against prayerlessness. This is because if the Law preaches against prayerlessness, it would actually stir prayerlessness!

Do not make the promise void

For if they which are of the law be heirs, faith is made void, and the promise made of none effect:
Romans 4:14

If we expect answers to prayer because we follow some rule or Law we make the promise of God of none effect. If your prayer life is law-driven, your praying is not sustained by promise but by your performance. If I believe that God answers prayers but does not answer mine because I do not measure up, that belief voids the promise. Christ is the promise of God. He is also the answer to my prayers. A fellow has all the answers to prayers that he'll ever need because he has the Son (2 Cor. 1:20). Jesus is God telling me YES! Everything is yours because of the promise of God. The prayer that we pray does not make anything ours. The grace of God teaches us that prayer is based on the foundation of already existing answers in Christ and prayer is a means of our receiving from God's wondrous provision. Understanding this relationship between our prayers and answers is pivotal. We acknowledge that the answers already exist within the promise. The law-driven mindset on the other hand maintains that the answers are non-existent and that God creates the answer in response to our praying. This anti-grace mindset sees prayer as a vehicle for convincing God that we are deserving of the answers.

Praying with yourself

And he spake this parable unto certain which trusted in themselves that they were righteous, and despised others: Two men went up into the temple to pray; the one a Pharisee, and the other a publican. The Pharisee stood and prayed thus with himself, God, I thank thee, that I am not as other men are, extortioners, unjust, adulterers, or even as this publican. I fast twice in the week, I give tithes of all that I possess. And the publican, standing afar off, would not lift up so much as his eyes unto heaven, but smote upon his breast, saying, God be merciful to me a sinner. I tell you, this man went down to his house justified rather than the other: for every one that exalteth himself shall be abased; and he that humbleth himself shall be exalted.
Luke 18:9-14

The law is good when used lawfully (1 Tim. 1:8). This means that the Law can be used unlawfully. The Law appeals to the flesh and not the human spirit. The Law makes sin come alive and it was designed to condemn anyone who trusts in self for salvation (Rom 3:19). Fleshly ruled folks, like the Pharisee, abuse the Law by trying to use it as a basis for receiving from God. A man that says, "I am so good, God has to answer my prayers" has actually said enough to betray his ignorance about the nature of the Law. He thinks that he has said that his observance of the law should invoke a blessing but what he does not know is that the Law works as a whole and must be obeyed fully as a whole. If you break one little bit of it but keep 99.99% of it, you have still broken the Law! It is unlawful to break portions of the Law and yet base your expectancy of answers on another part of the Law. Such a lifestyle attracts a curse, for anyone desiring to live by the Law is open to the curse except he fulfills every tiny requirement of the Law (Galatians 3:10)!

The Pharisee is morally impeccable. There is nothing wrong with excellent morals. It gives you a good name in the community as well as credibility in your relationship with others, which is a good thing! Good works also take opportunity away from satan. It would be unlawful for a morally cool person to think that their moral purity qualifies them before God. You have fallen from grace if you expect God to hear you in prayer because you are morally cool. Expect God to hear you because you are in Christ Jesus who has made you righteous.

Jesus shocks us with a scenario where the publican is more effective in prayer than the Pharisee. The Pharisee, though morally good, places his faith in his own morals, while the publican believes in God's mercy. Clearly the publican is not a paragon of virtues. Jesus shows that the legalistic mindset of the self-righteous person prevents them from receiving answers to prayer. It is faulty to reason that God answers the prayers of a moral person more than the prayers of an immoral person.

People who reason that their good works qualifies them before God are often quick to criticize others. The Pharisee spirit is a self-righteous one. It is impossible to find self-righteous people who do not despise others. Self-righteous people are unable to receive God's gift of righteousness within their spirit man. Their standard allows them despise others while excusing themselves. They are forever trying to win God's approval, therefore finding it hard to approve of others. They are "comparing themselves with themselves"; therefore, they are lacking in God's wisdom (2 Cor. 10.12). Wise people find that God has accepted them in Christ. He has accepted others also.

According to Jesus, people who are self-righteous and despising of others also pray. We cannot therefore conclude that just because we pray, the very act of praying confers on us a sainthood, which aligns our attitudes with God and with His Word. Prayer itself might prove that we are unscriptural.

The Pharisee stood and prayed thus with himself

This Pharisee thought that he was thanking God. It is true he said, "I thank thee" but he was unaware that thanksgiving is not merely in the use of the word "thanks" in prayer. Thanksgiving is an attitude of praise because of Jesus. Once you compare yourself with others, thanksgiving is dead. Even if your words are right, if the reason for thanksgiving is not based on something accomplished in Christ, you are not really giving thanks the Bible way.

The Pharisee was supremely conscious of the publican and of his own works. He was not conscious of God.

That Pharisee's prayer did not have its foundation in God at all, though he repeatedly used the word "God". Mentioning God in prayer does not mean the prayer is godly. A prayer that trusts in the relative goodness of our morals compared to that of other people is not prayer at all. In the New Covenant, if you pray without acknowledging that God accepts you in Christ, you destroy the effectiveness of your prayers.

That Pharisee thought that he was praying to God but according to Jesus, he was not. The Pharisee was praying with himself! Thus it is possible to speak Christianese, go through the motions of prayer and actually not be praying.

At best you are praying with yourself!

God be merciful to me a sinner.
Luke 18:13b

God looks for every excuse in the book to answer prayers! God does not consult the general religious community before determining that your prayers should be answered. The Pharisee is convinced that the publican's prayers cannot be answered. Thankfully, God does not factor in what others think before His mercy shines through. Just because you think someone is undeserving of answered prayer does not mean that their prayer would not be answered. The publican relied on God's mercy. It was Prophet Jonah who said of God, "I knew you were sheer grace and mercy, not easily angered, rich in love, and ready at the drop of a hat to turn your plans of punishment into a program of forgiveness" (Jonah 4:2b The Message).

This publican's prayer was much shorter than the Pharisee's prayer. It was not lengthy but it was effective. That publican recognized his need for a savior. When we received the salvation of God, we received all things.

Both the publican and the Pharisee stood up in prayer, yet the publican was effective while the Pharisee was not; it was therefore not about posture in prayer. A fellow could skip, stand or kneel in prayer all he wants. If he prioritizes his posture above the mercy of God, he forfeits the mercy and prevents himself from experiencing God. Posture in prayer is inconsequential until you find someone silly enough to place spiritual importance on it.

I fast twice in the week, I give tithes of all that I possess.
Luke 18:12

There is a place for fasting but it is not a means of getting God to answer your prayers. This Pharisee thought that the frequency of his fast scores points with God. There is nothing wrong with fasting twice a week if you so choose but it wins no medals with God. Expecting God to hear your prayers because you are accurate, faithful and punctual with your offerings and tithes will rob you of effectiveness in prayer because that is wrong thinking. Wrong thinking crowds out the mercy of God.

Giving and receiving – God's way

You crazy Galatians! Did someone put a hex on you? Have you taken leave of your senses? Something crazy has happened, for it's obvious that you no longer have the crucified Jesus in clear focus in your lives. His sacrifice on the cross was certainly set before you clearly enough.
Galatians 3:1 (The Message)

O you dear idiots of Galatia, who saw Jesus Christ the crucified so plainly, who has been casting a spell over you? I will ask you one simple question: did you receive the Spirit of God by trying to keep the Law or by believing the message of the Gospel? Surely you can't be so idiotic as to think that a man begins his spiritual life in the Spirit and then completes it by reverting to outward observances?
Galatians 3:1 -3 (JB Phillips)

Paul felt it was crazy and idiotic to attempt to receive from God on any other foundation but the finished work of Christ. Don't be a dear spiritual idiot! Learn to enjoy your privileges in Christ.

Paul is discussing giving (Gal 3:5) and receiving (Gal 3:2). That is, how do we receive from God and how does God give to us. In this conversation, Paul links both. They are two sides of the same coin. In the first instance, he starts with how we receive from God. Do we receive from God by observing the Law or by faith? Those who had been exposed to Judaism amongst them will rightly say they were familiar with receiving from God through the observance of the Law. The nature of the question shows that Paul intended for the answer to be totally different. In other words, he wants the correct answer to be the one that says that we receive from God through faith and not through the observance of the Law. The implication is that anyone under the New Covenant who tries to receive from God on the basis of observance of Laws is actually under a spell. That believer is bewitched! I know that is a rather strong terminology. This clearly is not something to take lightly. His language is robust and he spares no punches as he seeks to free these folks from idiotic receiving. We receive answers to prayer from God not because of what we have done right or otherwise. We receive because of what Jesus has done right. Even when thoughts of guilt attack our heart, we let the Word kill satan's accusation while we approach our Father thankfully on the basis of His Word.

After establishing how the receiving side should work, Paul looks at it differently from the other side of the coin, the giving side. When God gives the Spirit and works miracles in the church, does He do it by our observance of the Law or by the hearing of faith? God does not give to us by bargain. He does not do deals with us. He gives without the Law or the observation of the Law in mind. For instance, since God has given Christ as salvation, we do not ask Him to save the lost. We pray for the one who hears the good news to believe it so that by believing he might receive that, which is already provided in God. Our focus in prayer today turns from telling God to do something, since He has already given, to helping that person receive faith by hearing what God has done.

Stay practical

And the LORD said unto Moses, Go, get thee down; for thy people, which thou broughtest out of the land of Egypt, have corrupted themselves:
Exodus 32:7

Moses was on the mountain with God in a time of intense communion. While Moses and God were in conversation, the children of Israel were in disarray. God noticed it. It wasn't God's place to settle that matter directly. The people had a leader whose job it was to handle such things. God was going to intervene in these affairs through the Leader. God informed Moses and basically told Moses to go down to the people. Thankfully Moses is unlike most religious people who in a similar scenario would have insisted on continuing with their "alone" time with God while they leave it to God to take control.

In this scenario, God demonstrated that good government was more beneficial for that society than Moses' continuing in prayer on the mountaintop. Clearly, if the children of Israel were not in disarray, Moses should seek to maximise that kind of alone time with God on the mountaintop. Moses would be praying beyond God's ability if he prayed to God to sort out what was happening down there so Moses could stay on the mountain. Asking God to take control of the things He has given you control over is asking God to do something beyond His ability. The most spiritual thing for Moses to do in that instance was to climb down that mountain and offer leadership to his people.

God is practical. Therefore real spirituality is also practical. Some people are not mature enough to hear God tell them to leave a time of intense prayer in order to attend to things in the natural realm, which if left untended could give satan the advantage. They then wonder why in spite of so much prayer, the level of pandemonium and chaos in their world is not diminished.

Let's do a thought experiment:

Let's imagine a woman, the mother of two children, one is a five year old and the other is two years old. Her husband is out of town on a business assignment and she's decided to set aside extended times of daily prayer after listening to some fire-brand preacher on TV. She chooses a time when she leaves the children unsupervised just after bringing them in from school. She anticipates that the Lord will see her heart and reward her by taking care of those children supernaturally. She declares that just as the angels cooked supernatural food for Elijah, God would send His angels to cook a warm dinner for the children while she discusses with God in prayer. She discovers that no matter how much she prays, the level of pandemonium in the house just keeps increasing. She thinks the devil is at work. She is correct in more ways than she realizes. While in prayer she finds her mind straying towards the kids and continues to bind the satanic distraction that is hindering her from concentrating on her two-hour prayer marathon. Her children have not eaten, are still in their school uniforms and are generally restless. She is perplexed as to why she is unable to concentrate in prayer. Her supposed distraction is not satanic. Her human spirit is preventing Her from harvesting her folly.

The devil was at work, not in the pandemonium caused by hungry children who are missing the sweet presence of their mother but in the foolishness that caused this woman to abdicate her parenting responsibilities to God! Asking God to do what He has commissioned you to do in His Word is not spiritual on any level. Her spirit is fed up with her folly and will have none of the nonsense she is trying to practice in the name of spirituality. True spirituality in that scenario helps the children unwind after a long day at school. In giving food to those children and helping them settle down, she is serving the Lord. The Lord considers time spent with the children supplying them with leadership and the sweet presence of a mother as a direct fulfilment of the Word. The desire to leave the children in their school uniform and in a disruptive state is a misrepresentation of the very God that she thinks she is praying to. That kind of tradition will make the Word of God of none effect and expose the children to chaos and disorder.

Illusions of prayer

Some years ago while I was praying, I heard God ask me a question that got me somewhat perplexed with God. The question was deceptively simple, "What are you doing?"

Surely it was obvious I was praying, why on earth would God be asking me the obvious?

I brushed God's question aside and kept on praying for a while, until it finally dawned on me that God had not said, "Sekou, what are you praying about?"

He had asked me, "What are you doing?"

I thought that I was praying, but God could not find a name for what I was doing. It was anything but prayer!

Any time God asks me questions, it is not for His education but for mine. He wanted to point out to me that even though

I thought I was praying, He did not think so. I had some unlearning to do. Unlearning can be tough. It is easier to cast out devils than to cast out traditions! Prayer is not immune from right and wrong thinking. People who think and reason wrong tend to pray wrong.

Prayer is not designed to inform God

Be not ye therefore like unto them: for your Father knoweth what things ye
have need of, before ye ask him.
Matthew 6:8

When Jesus taught on prayer, He first spent time discussing what prayer is not. God already knows what you need before you ask him. Our asking is not so as to inform Him. It is a way of releasing the power within God's Word to meet your need. There is nothing wrong with discussing your challenges with God but that does not bring about a change of your circumstances. God wants you to tell your circumstance what He has said instead of you telling Him the things your circumstance is saying to you!

Hypocrites love to pray

And when thou prayest, thou shalt not be as the hypocrites are: for they
love to pray standing in the synagogues and in the corners of the streets,
that they may be seen of men. Verily I say unto you, They have their
reward.
Matthew 6:5

Years ago, I thought King James English was a heavenly dialect. When I prophesied, I did so in as near "King James" as I could. Afterwards, I would continue teaching in my everyday English flow. Unconsciously I thought that the KJV-speak was a seal

RIGHT & WRONG PRAYING

of genuineness. Some people still suppose that praying in King James English is extra icing on the cake. There is nothing wrong with praying in "King James" but it is hypocrisy if you adopt that style because you think God likes King James phonetics. Praying in flowery language because of others who are present is a display of hypocrisy. If you pray publicly because you want others to know you are a person of prayer, the answer to your prayer is that many people will know that you are a person of prayer. Prayer derives its true meaning not from the use of correct terminology but the heart motive of the one praying. This is true of anything that has to do with the heart.

Jesus tells us that Hypocrites love to pray. Effectiveness in prayer is more than just loving to pray. If hypocrisy is in the heart, prayer becomes an outlet for the release of hypocrisy. The Pharisees pray to be seen by others as people of prayer. They could have used that time of prayer for other things but they set it aside for prayer, which is commendable, it's just that they were let down by poor attitudes in prayer. It's like those who pray for a set number of hours each day, just so they can also tell their friends that they do not wilt easily in prayer. Their prayer life only gathers momentum in the presence of others who they need to see them as people of prayer. They are paying a great price to be noticed of men. Their reward is that they will obtain bragging rights before others. They also get their time in the spot light when they tell others how long they are able to pray for. Their result is that others see, acknowledge and celebrate them but their prayer is with themselves and not with God.

Jesus did not permit Disciples copy Elijah

A lot of what Jesus taught about prayer strips away false ideologies about prayer. Jesus did not just add to what these precious folks already knew about prayer. Wrong thinking when mixed with praying produces frustrated Christians and fanciful traditions. His method was to help us learn what prayer is by clearly showcasing what it is not.

And it came to pass, when the time was come that he should be received up, he stedfastly set his face to go to Jerusalem, And sent messengers before his face: and they went, and entered into a village of the Samaritans, to make ready for him. And they did not receive him, because his face was as though he would go to Jerusalem And when his disciples James and John saw this, they said, Lord, wilt thou that we command fire to come down from heaven, and consume them, even as Elias did? But he turned, and rebuked them, and said, Ye know not what manner of spirit ye are of. For the Son of man is not come to destroy men's lives, but to save them. And they went to another village.
Luke 9:51-56

The Samaritans were not going to receive Jesus because of existing ethnic tensions between the Jews and the Samaritans. The disciples of Jesus were going to teach the Samaritan "infidels" a lesson by praying down fire to consume the whole lot "even as Elijah did"!

The disciples had their ethnic biases. They were trying to find scriptural justification for their violent disposition towards the Samaritans. Calling down fire from heaven was the signature style of Elijah. He called fire down at least three times; once on Mount Carmel in the defeat of Baal's prophets and twice on soldiers. The disciples felt they had three "witnesses" for this in scripture.

What was Jesus' response to these Bible-quoting bloodthirsty prayerful men? He rebuked them, thus disallowing His followers from calling down fire from heaven upon men. There are many Christians today who did not get this memo from Jesus. Elijah in his day had used the power at his disposal to release wrath. Jesus wants us to use the power to release mercy. Elijah was angry but God was not.

While the disciples had biblical precedence, they did not know that one could correctly quote the Bible and yet remain grossly ignorant of God's true intent. Our uncertainty about God's goodness causes us to entertain schizophrenic ideas about God and to mistake our wrath and violence for His. To put it bluntly, one cannot see Jesus as the true exegesis of God and in the same vein claim that God rubber-stamped the violence in the Old Testament.

The most dangerous foundation for killing others is that which is supposedly based on the Bible. The disciples were projecting their own vengeful image of God onto their reading of the Bible. They wanted Jesus to validate their desire to have those Samaritans dead. Some Christians today nurture their own man-made vengeful biases and find pretext for "killing" others without discerning the intent of the Holy Spirit. The letter killed them and they killed others. Jesus never killed anyone nor does He endorse the killing of others who we disagree with. He came to give life. While the gospel contains no record of Jesus using the fire of God to deal with His adversaries, His disciples felt that Jesus was capable of the same unimaginable brutality that they were capable of towards other men. God must be in shock when He ponders the things the church think He is capable of. They suppose that these are the days of Elijah but we know that a greater than Elijah has come! Has Jesus changed? Is He now permitting His disciples to sort out things Elijah-style while He did not permit it during His earth walk?

Rather than following the example of Prophet Elijah, Jesus expected His disciples to discern the real spirit of Jesus' character. We remember that though Elijah tried to represent God as best as he could, he never saw God (John 1:18). We should look past

Elijah and gaze into the face of Jesus in order to get the true revelation of the Father God. Jesus correctly interprets God. Moreover Jesus is Lord, not Elijah! The principle in prayer is that we first discern what God wants done by looking to Jesus as the template and then pray its manifestation into being. Our prayers are to be guided by the spirit of love and not the spirit of violence.

This episode involving Jesus and His disciples show that even if there is "scriptural" evidence, a literal interpretation should be avoided if such interpretation leads us to think that God wants us to use prayer to bring about the death of men. According to the Lord Jesus, the disciples were ignorant of the nature of God's Spirit by trying to bring about the death of those Samaritans through some heavenly fire. The Lord's intention is for us to discern by the recreated spirit how to apply a portion of scripture. Obviously, if all that God wanted us to function by was the reading of the Bible in a literal way, there would have been absolutely no reason for providing the new birth for our spirits, the indwelling of the Holy Spirit and our communion with the Father God. He wants a living relationship, not static pages of the letter, which kills. In the true sense, Jesus was the "Elijah" calling down fire upon the bigotry and wrong thoughts of those disciples. We don't call down fire to kill people. We pray down fire to destroy our own spiritual blindness and irreverent thoughts.

Hearing the beloved son

And as he prayed, the fashion of his countenance was altered, and his raiment was white and glistering. And, behold, there talked with him two men, which were Moses and Elias: Who appeared in glory, and spake of his decease which he should accomplish at Jerusalem. But Peter and they that were with him were heavy with sleep: and when they were awake,

they saw his glory, and the two men that stood with him. And it came to pass, as they departed from him, Peter said unto Jesus, Master, it is good for us to be here: and let us make three tabernacles; one for thee, and one for Moses, and one for Elias: not knowing what he said. While he thus spake, there came a cloud, and overshadowed them: and they feared as they entered into the cloud. And there came a voice out of the cloud, saying, This is my beloved Son: hear him.
Luke 9:29-35

This simply told story is a scriptural puzzle. For starters, How did Moses, a man held under the bars of death in that prison house, show up on earth at a point in time before the resurrection of Jesus? Moses had suddenly died at the peak of his powers without any health conditions in a valley in the land of Moab (Deut. 34:6), well over a thousand years before this event and was gathered to his people (Deut. 32:50). There was no obvious reason for his death. It seems time ran out for him at the age of 120 years (Deut. 34:7).

Some remarkable things happened following Moses' death. In an unusual move, God buried Moses. Moses' body must have special significance in God's plans. I don't believe that was done to prevent the Jews from worshipping Moses. The Jews knew the burial place of Abraham and David (Acts 2:29) and did not worship either, though both are revered. Michael had a dispute with satan over Moses' body (Jude v.9). Since this enigmatic dispute is about Moses' body, I believe it either relates to its burial or the waking of that body. It is likely that Satan felt that he had the title deed to the bodies of men because they were captives in the house of death. There are those who suggest that Archangel Michael was attempting to take Moses' body out of the earth in a type of rapture. Elijah's transport to heaven in angelic chariots happened in the same valley where Moses' body had been buried. They say that after Michael's dispute over

Moses, he resurrected Moses' body and put it in the chariot that was later used as Elijah's transport to heaven. Even then all these would have happened on credit since the Lord Jesus had not yet provided any redemption; therefore, had not yet released those under captivity (See Ephesians 4:8). It was not until after Jesus rose from the dead that the bodies of saints rose out of the grave and appeared to many (Mt. 27:52-53).

And as they came down from the mountain, Jesus charged them, saying, Tell the vision to no man, until the Son of man be risen again from the dead.
Matthew 17:9

Matthew's retelling of Moses and Elijah appearing on that mountain gives us a clue. As the disciples came down the physical mountain, the Lord Jesus described the whole experience as a vision. This is a spiritual vision. This means that Moses and Elijah were not actually physically present on earth at that point in time. If some other person had been on that mountain, he would not have seen Moses and Elijah. The degree of glory manifested had been so strong that these disciples fell down under the power of God (Mt. 17:6). They remained under the grip of that power until Jesus used His touch to release them (Mt 17:7).

This episode on the mountain happened just before this Samaritan incidence of disciples desiring to call down fire upon enemies. Peter, James and John had been up a physical mountain with Jesus. As the Lord Jesus began to pray so much spiritual power was released that triggered something profound. Jesus, Peter, James and John were all transported to the future via a spiritual vision where all saw Moses and Elijah.

Peter recalled this episode when he wrote the following:

> *For we have not followed cunningly devised fables, when we made known unto you the power and coming of our Lord Jesus Christ, but were eyewitnesses of his majesty. For he received from God the Father honour and glory, when there came such a voice to him from the excellent glory, This is my beloved Son, in whom I am well pleased. And this voice which came from heaven we heard, when we were with him in the holy mount.*
>
> *2 Peter 1:16-18*

Whatever Peter is talking about here will sound like a far-fetched tale to the typical hearer; this is why he tells them that it was not the product of an active imagination. Notice that Peter said, "we", referring to himself, James and John, as eyewitnesses of Jesus' majesty. He pinpointed this event to have taken place when God's voice said, "This is my beloved Son, in whom I am well pleased". This corresponds to the transfiguration of Jesus on the mountain, which is recorded in Luke 9. According to Peter, the voice came from excellent glory. This is the glory of that cloud that enveloped them, while they were on the mount. This mount is not necessarily the physical mountain in Israel that they had climbed that day but a reference to what Peter calls the holy mount. This holy mount would be in the heavenly plane in the spirit realm (Rev 21). It would appear that the Lord Jesus, Moses, Elijah, Peter, James and John were all transported into the future, into heaven, where they all saw Jesus in His future glorified body upon the holy mountain in the heavenly realm (See Rev 21.10). This sounded like fables to Peter's hearers. Peter assured them it was truth of the highest order.

Moses who had been dead over 1,500 years did not come to the earth to have conversations with the living. Jesus took Peter, James and John up an unnamed physical mountain from which they were transported up a spiritual mountain to hear God validate Jesus as the authentic meaning of all scripture. All that were caught up in that spiritual vision heard God say "This is my beloved son: Hear him". Moses and Elijah are a reference to the Law and the Prophets, which were spiritually deficient in conveying the true intention of God because they were addressed to men who were limited by spiritual death. The Father is saying, "First hear Jesus, then you understand all things including Moses and Elijah". Wherever the disciples find a conflict between Jesus and Elijah, they should go with Jesus who would shed light on all things. If Elijah could overhear Jesus rebuking the disciples for desiring to call down fire from heaven upon men, Elijah would have sided in with Jesus against the disciples who tried to copy his methods. Elijah acted as he best knew how with the light that he had. On a lighter note, Elijah would have called down fire upon them for trying to call down fire upon these Samaritans!

In calling down fire, Elijah's condition was, "if I be a man of God". Elijah's sign was, "let fire come down". Is this the fire of God? Continue to ponder and so doing learn the difference between Man of God and Son of Man.

The scriptures that depict violence are not teaching us to do likewise to those who do not believe God. They teach us how not to relate to our neighbours. Put yourself in the shoes of those Old Testament saints, If like them you had a near zero revelation concerning a being as evil as satan, you'll end up attributing everything in your world to God whether good or evil. You'll think God was at work when in fact it was satan. You would also end up ignorantly describing the voice of satan as God speaking to you. In that scenario, you would interpret satan's threats to be God's anger. You would then try to appease an angry God, when you should be rebuking and resisting satan the thief who steals and destroys (John 10:10). People call down the fire of God not knowing from whom the fire really comes and to whom the destruction and death should be attributed. Since the writer of Hebrews says that satan had the power of death by which he exercised lordship over those who were held in bondage through fear (Heb. 2:14), where are the places in the Old Testament where this destructive tendency of satan is on display?

8

WHO IS IN CONTROL?

To ask the question, "Who is in the driver's seat concerning the affairs of this earth" is no theoretical question. It is rooted in reality and human experience. To a religious person, this is a no question for starters, for it seems fairly obvious that God is definitely in control of the earth. After all, He is the creator who can do as well as He pleases with the works of His own hands. In His Word, we find that He has set boundaries as to who He is, what He will do and how He operates.

Are we the helpless victims caught in the middle of a cosmic war that was not of our own making? If we will humbly approach God's Word and believe what God has revealed to us in His holy Word, we can have answers to our questions, though the answers might surprise us.

God will have all rule and authority

*Then cometh the end, when he shall have delivered up the kingdom to God,
even the Father; when he shall have put down all rule and all authority
and power. For he must reign, till he hath put all enemies under his feet.*
1 Corinthians 15:24-25

According to Paul, Christ has to first put down all rule and all
authority before He delivers the kingdom up to God. Though
people shy away from this, the fact is that God is not in control
of all rule and authority on this earth. We like to think that God is
ruling in the kingdom now but the Bible says that God Himself
is waiting for the kingdom to be delivered to Him by Jesus. The
reason why Jesus cannot yet deliver the kingdom to the Father is
because there are rules and authority and power that need to be
put to an end but have not yet been put to an end. It stands to
reason that this rule that needs to be put to an end is not God's
rule, for why would Christ put God's rule to an end only to then
deliver it up to God again? The rule that needs to be put to an
end is other than God's. It is a realm of authority that is not
under God's jurisdiction right now. When Jesus puts these rules
and authority to an end, the kingdom would have been delivered
to God who will then have all rule, all authority and all power.

It is at the end that Jesus delivers the kingdom to our Father God.
When we read that Christ must reign till He has put all enemies
under His feet, what do we make of that statement? Does the
Bible not teach that Christ is already exalted far above all rules
and authority as well as every name that is named (Eph. 1:21)?
Did Christ not say after His resurrection that all power had been
given unto him (Mt 28:18)? The truth is that Jesus has conquered
satan (Col. 2:15). All things have already been put under Jesus,
however because of our neglect of the redemption that Jesus
has provided we don't yet see everything put under Jesus (Heb.
2:8-9). Few are enforcing the conquest of satan today.

When the Bible speaks of the feet in, "till he hath put all enemies under his feet", feet is symbolic language for the body of Christ on earth. Jesus is head over all things for the benefit of His Church, which is His body (Eph. 1:22-23). Right now, the Lord Jesus Himself is not directly enforcing satan's defeat because if Jesus directly does anything more than what He has already done, He will bring the curtain to a close on the state of affairs on this earth. Christ has not yet directly exercised this authority and power that puts all enemies under the church yet. The only reason why He delays is in the hope that as many men as possible will receive salvation (2 Pet. 3:9). He waits patiently for the fruit of the earth, the precious souls of men (Jam. 5:7). Today Jesus exercises that authority through His church but the church has largely not enforced His victory over satan, therefore satan goes about not yet subdued. In the absence of Jesus on the earth, the church is tasked with bringing satan under control. Men continue to give satan authority today by yielding to him (Rom. 6:16). We are the ones as members of His body that are doing something about satan and his works today in the name of Jesus. The authority that satan functions through on earth today is the permission he gets through people who do not resist him steadfastly in the faith. It is only as the Church resists satan in faith, that satan's wriggle room shrinks on the earth.

For he hath put all things under his feet. But when he saith all things are put under him, it is manifest that he is excepted, which did put all things under him. And when all things shall be subdued unto him, then shall the Son also himself be subject unto him that put all things under him, that God may be all in all.
1 Corinthians 15:27-28

This makes sense once we recall that in the beginning, God was all in all on this earth. The Bible shows that God began to delegate authority and power by investing it in Adam (Gen. 1:26). God himself was not under the control of anyone. During the period when the authority and power is given to others, it is not in God's possession; for if it is, there would be no need for the Son to come on the scene, reclaim the authority and power, put an end to them and then return all authority and power to the Father.

The implication is that all things are not right now subject to the Father! Authority will go full cycle and return back to God who delegated the authority in the first place. One day, the Son, as the Last Adam, will subject Himself as well as all the rules He has subdued to God. This is not yet the case because the Son has not ended all authority and power. Thus right now, God is not yet all in all. There is coming a time, when He will definitely be all in all. The implication is that there is a lot happening today that is not proceeding from God!

1 Corinthians 15 shows that there are only two men that God reckons with. The full history of humanity is summarized in these two men - The two Adams. The first Adam came into the Garden of Eden and was given rule and authority by God over this earth (Gen. 1:26) and the Second Adam, who is also the Last Adam, came forth as man's redeemer. This last Adam will subdue all rule and authority to God. It is as man, the Last Adam that Jesus will enforce the end of all rule and authority and it is also as a man that He will subject Himself back to God, thus handing back to God all authority and power.

God remains the owner but He has given the rulership

Since it is at the end that the man Jesus Christ returns all rule and authority to God, there will likely be clues at the beginning about God releasing authority to another.

You ask yourself,

"Who did God give authority and power to and when did He do this?"

A brief history of authority starts in Genesis:

In the beginning God created the heaven and the earth.
Genesis 1.1

God is the creator of the heaven and the earth. In the beginning, before He delegated authority to any other, He determined what happened on this earth and when it happened.

And God said, Let us make man in our image, after our likeness: and let them have dominion over the fish of the sea, and over the fowl of the air, and over the cattle, and over all the earth, and over every creeping thing that creepeth upon the earth. Genesis 1:26

Then by His own design, God gave the rule and authority of the whole earth to man! He did this right at the beginning, when He introduced His man into the earth. Man has always possessed the God-given rule and authority of this earth (Ps. 8:6). Man did not usurp this authority. God gave it to man as a gift. God gave authority solely to man and not to any other being. He gave the rule and authority to man without any terms or conditions whatsoever. It was really unconditional! God could have given conditions and small-print type qualifications if He wanted to but that was not the type of rulership that God wanted for His man.

God sees man as the ruler of the earth

The heaven, even the heavens, are the LORD's: but the earth hath he given to the children of men.
Psalm 115.16

Both the heaven and the earth are the Lord's. The ownership has never changed. God made man ruler of the earth. God willed for the earth to have a ruler other than Himself. Man was not made ruler of the heavens. The earth is man's realm of authority while God retained authority over the heavenly realms. God gave to man the rulership and authority of the earth without any strings attached. This is what it means when the Bible says that God gave, or more accurately assigned, the earth to the children of men.

You have put him in charge of everything you made; everything is put under his authority:
Psalm 8.6 (TLB)

The Psalmist said, "You put everything under his feet". God had given to man absolute authority over the works of His hands without adding any conditions. It was a gift to man.

God gifted Adam with the power of choice. We like to feel in control of our choices but the only choice we are in control of is the choice of what to yield to. Once we yield to something, we are really no longer free even though we think that we are (Rom. 6:16). We are responding to whatever influence that we allow in our lives. Adam should have gifted that power of choice back to God by using this power to choose God forever. We train ourselves to learn the secret of recognizing and choosing God's will all the time. When we do not choose God, we crowd Him out of our domain. Adam's choice of anything other than God is an abuse of the intent behind the giving of that power.

The visible and the invisible dimensions

Who is the image of the invisible God, the firstborn of every creature:
For by him were all things created, that are in heaven, and that are in
earth, visible and invisible, whether they be thrones, or dominions, or
principalities, or powers: all things were created by him, and for him:
Colossians 1:15-16

The Bible says, "In the beginning God created the heaven and the earth". This means that God created the visible and the invisible dimensions. There are other dimensions asides the earth. The visible and invisible dimensions abide under God-ordained authority. God Himself operates in the invisible dimension. Man is not required to govern the invisible dimension. Today God is not the one governing the visible dimension. God does not govern the affairs of this earth. He gave to man the dominion over the visible dimension. There are spiritual beings in the invisible realm and their primary sphere of operation is in the invisible realm. These spiritual beings do not govern the earth.

Jesus gives us more clues as to the parties that play a part in the happenings on this earth.

Who is ruling what?

The thief cometh not, but for to steal, and to kill, and to destroy: I
am come that they might have life, and that they might have it more
abundantly.
John 10:10

When Jesus said, "I am come that you may have life and that more abundantly", He was not speaking as God but as a man. There is a thief on the earth. This thief is one of the players on the earth. Satan is the murderer from the beginning who is the thief who steals, kills and destroys. You do not have to sin personally in order for the thief to operate. He will be unruly if allowed. After all, he is a thief. Since the thief kills and yet not all are dead, the effectiveness of the thief is not fully down to the thief alone. This causes us to ask, "When the effect of the thief is not felt, is it down to God?" If it was solely up to God, why do we not see the thief restrained one hundred percent of the time?

Folks intuitively think that it must be God's job to stop the thief. They assume that since God is the creator and the owner of this earth, therefore He is in full control of happenings on it. If we follow that logic given the evil that we see on the earth, this means that God fluctuates in the quality of protection that He delivers. What kind of control is that?

The scriptures give yet another option. This option does not place responsibility for the affairs of this earth at either the thief's door or at God's door. Jesus implied it when He said, "Be it unto you according to your faith" (Mt. 9:29). You would have expected Him to say, "Be it unto you according to God's intervention and God's will", but that's not what He said! By saying, "according to your faith" (Mk. 5:34), Jesus affirms the primal role that our faith plays in the outcomes we permit on the earth. Since God gave man the rulership of the earth, it is not surprising that man is the singular most important factor determining outcomes on the earth. The reason why it appears that both God and The thief vary in effectiveness is because man varies in exercising his responsibility to resist satan in faith so as to cause him to flee (1 Peter 5:9, James 4:7).

God has given us His own faith and then told us to use that faith to receive outcomes and use our authority to enforce them. He does not tell us to ask Him to move our mountains (Mark 11:23). The moving of mountains is under our control. While it is true that there are mountains in our path, we are not to continue to entertain the idea that it is up to God whether the mountains move or not. Jesus shows us that there is direct relationship between faith and authority (Mt. 8:9-10). Bible faith goes hand in hand with authority.

The ruler of this world

We know that we are children of God and that all the rest of the world around us is under Satan's power and control.
1 John 5:19 (Living Bible)

Believers are not under the dominion of satan (Col. 1:13). Satan's power is derived from darkness. He is enhanced wherever the light of God's Word is rejected which results in darkness. The people under the spell of satan have authority. They have no light with which to exercise that authority for their own good, so satan uses their combined authority to establish a footprint on the earth.

Satan himself does not directly do all the havoc on the earth, it is people in positions of power who let him function through the darkness in their reasoning and philosophies (Eph. 4:17-19). When people under the spell of darkness receive the light of God's Word they are no longer within satan's embrace but under the Lordship of Jesus (Acts 26:18). Men who receive the light of life in their candles become masters over satan (Ps. 18:28). Jesus himself had mastery over satan not because He was God but because as a man He only acknowledged the light of God so satan had nothing in Him (John 14:30).

Now is the judgment of this world: now shall the prince of this world be cast out.
John 12:31
But if our gospel be hid, it is hid to them that are lost: In whom the god

of this world hath blinded the minds of them which believe not, lest the light of the glorious gospel of Christ, who is the image of God, should shine unto them.
2 Corinthians 4:3-4

Jesus referred to satan as the prince or the ruler of this world (John 14:30, 16:11). God did not make satan the prince of this world. God created Lucifer a cherub angel, who later rebelled and obtained this princely status from men who love the darkness more than the light. Jesus spoke of casting satan out as prince because Adam and all men had made him a prince in the first place through their choices. Satan is really man-made. He derives his powers from men yielding to him to obey him (Rom 6:16).

When a man receives Jesus as his Lord and his life, satan is cast out as prince over that believing one (Acts 26:18). His only access is then deception (2 Cor. 11:3). He functions as a prince over deceived people, whose minds are blinded to the truth of God's Word. When Paul refers to satan as the god of this world, that world refers to those who are lost. The world is a system of influence sustained by those who are not governed by the gospel. Satan rules over those who have not received eternal life. The reception of eternal life into the human spirit is actually a transfer out of satan's authority (Col 1.13).

The pattern seems to be that only rulers can make other rulers. God, who is Himself a ruler, was qualified to make man a ruler. We have to ask ourselves, "Who made satan a ruler?" there are only two candidates who qualify – God or man for these are the two rulers we see in the first chapters of Genesis.

As the original ruler of both the heavens and the earth, God made man ruler of the earth, while He retained the rulership of heaven. Man's rulership is not man-made, it is God's design. When Jesus walked this earth, He referred to satan as the ruler of this world who would be judged and cast out (John 12:31)! Jesus acknowledges that there are three rulers. Two are original and the third is derived. God and man rule in the invisible and visible dimensions respectively and because men yield to satan, satan is called the ruler of this world. He rules the world through the cumulative of the authority of men who yield to him.

This has been delivered unto me

Behold, I give unto you power to tread on serpents and scorpions, and over all the power of the enemy: and nothing shall by any means hurt you.
Luke 10.19

The Lord Jesus delegated His own authority to the disciples prior to His death and resurrection. They were not born again men. Their candle was not lit for they did not have the light of life within their spirits. Jesus Himself was not operating by delegated authority, for He was born without spiritual death. God had lit His candle; therefore He had authority in His very person. He operated by a resident anointing. Power was always available to flow through Him. The believer is also a son of God and a joint heir with Christ. Today we do not function by delegated authority.

When the Lord Jesus said, "nothing shall by any means hurt you", He implied that we do get hurt when we do not use the power at our disposal. The enemy uses the power at his disposal to hurt wherever man permits him. Man does not need to commit sin. If we are negligent about exercising our authority over the devil, we might find the enemy plundering us in various areas of life (Heb. 2:3). Many people think that the enemy only attacks because of sin. Therefore, they are perplexed when without any obvious sin, they find satan plundering them. Instead of fishing for sin in our lives, we should simply enforce our authority over all of satan's power to steal, kill and destroy. We have authority over and above all the power of the enemy. God does not hurt us. God has given us power. He won't use the power for us. We are to learn to command God's power by faith.

The enemy would have you believe that everything that happens to us on this earth comes to pass by God's will or His permission. In the first instance God does not need to permit anything since God is not the one in control of the earth. We already do a good job of permitting! God supplies the power that we can use to limit the enemy. The use of this power is up to us and not up to God. God is responsible for supplying you with power, while you are responsible for using it as the one in charge on earth!

And the devil, taking him up into an high mountain, shewed unto him all the kingdoms of the world in a moment of time. 6 And the devil said unto him, All this power will I give thee, and the glory of them: for that is delivered unto me; and to whomsoever I will I give it.
Luke 4:5-6

This conversation between the devil and the Lord Jesus happened before His death on the cross. It is shocking to the religious mind that Jesus did not dispute any of satan's assertions concerning authority.

Let's break down what satan said in Jesus' presence:

I have authority over all the kingdoms of the world.

I can give you (Jesus) this authority and the glory of the kingdoms.

This authority was not mine originally.

This authority has been delivered to me.

Satan stated the cold hard facts. Satan said these things to Jesus just after he had shown Jesus "all the kingdoms of the world".

Satan says that he can give to Jesus the authority over the "kingdoms of the world" which were given to him. He is stating the spiritual fact that authority can be transferred. Satan was speaking as the prince of this world. God did not make satan the prince of this world. Since only a ruler can make another ruler that leaves those that God had originally given authority to as the only other suspects. There is a God-given authority that God gave to man which ended up in satan's hands because someone other than God gave it to satan! God's mandate gives each man authority on this earth (Ps 115.16). Man mostly uses that authority to implement satan's ideas (Rom 6:16). This is the explanation of the princehood of satan. He derives it from men that he deceives.

Satan definitely has a kingdom but the kingdom is a kingdom of darkness (Colossians 1:13). Satan rules in darkness and ignorance. This kingdom consists of the cumulative authority of all those who reject the light of God's Word and are in rebellion against God. These people who submit to him are scattered all over the earth therefore satan exercises geo-political control across the earth because people who embrace darkness are scattered around the globe. He has accumulated this influence over thousands of years. It is a control he derives from people in those locations submitting to him individually (Rom 6:16). When those individuals receive the light of God's Word, satan's geo-political control shrinks. The people are translated out of the power of darkness into the kingdom of the Son as sons themselves. So it is rebellious people who reject the light together with the demons who constitute the power of satan which is the kingdom and power of darkness. People attract the effects of this kingdom on themselves by yielding to satan and rejecting the Word of God, which is the spiritual light that God shines.

These people individually hand over their realm of influence to satan. This is what was handed over to satan, firstly by Adam and Eve and by all men individually when they reject the light of God's Word and yield to satan.

Men who walk by the light of life do not yield any influence over to satan. Jesus handed nothing to satan. Remember that in the Genesis account, God did not give Adam dominion over other human beings but over the earth and the things in it. Therefore, Adam never got control over the kingdoms of this world from God. Adam could never have handed that over to satan simply because there were no kingdoms of people to rule when Adam fell! Every man has authority because God has never reversed the Genesis mandate, which gifted man with the rulership of this earth. Each man yields his own authority for satan's use as they buy into satan's lies. As a final masterstroke, satan then convinces men that they do not have authority.

God is honorable and not meddlesome. He gave man a rulership that gave man latitude within which man could act independent of God. Man then extended this to satan who also acts independent of God manipulating affairs on this earth through man's consent.

When Adam sinned in the garden, he was not acting on God's plan. He was acting independent of God. Man could act this way because he had been given unconditional authority. Man, by his actions had made a "home" for satan on the earth while crowding God out at the same time!

And I will put enmity between thee and the woman, and between thy seed and her seed; it shall bruise thy head, and thou shalt bruise his heel.
Genesis 3.15

In the scripture above, God speaks of the bruising of the head. He is addressing satan. Scholars tell us that the Hebrew word translated "head" here is the same as the one we would use when conveying the idea of the head of a company, thus it is better translated as the one in authority. The key thing to note here is that God admitted that something had transpired between Adam and satan that had changed both satan and man! Satan was now also a spiritual head, one who has authority over man in the kingdom of darkness as the god of this world. God did not cancel the whole thing and say, "This is not My plan, let's start over again by resetting the system". As to His personality and integrity, God is not one who goes back on what He has said. He does not alter what He says (Psalm 89.34). If He is going to retain His integrity and not become a fickle despot, He cannot go back on what He has said. This means He cannot use force to stop this deadly coalition between Adam and satan!

Adam had not used authority the way that God anticipated that man would use the authority that he had at his disposal. Satan now had access to that unconditional authority. God delivered it to Adam with no strings attached. In every single instance that God could have turned Adam into a puppet, God has honored His original transfer of authority to Adam.

That term "seed of the woman" should normally have been "seed of the man", since it is men that supply seed. God implies that the birth of Jesus would be a normal birth in that a woman would play a part but yet that birth would be special because the "seed" is not from a man. The seed of the woman that God spoke about was Jesus who emptied himself of His divine privileges and became a man. This prophecy means that a man is the solution of this earth. This is the way God thinks. We think God is the solution of the earth but God has designed an earth that is best resolved by a man.

We have found out that:

God transferred the authority of the earth to man without conditions.

Each man then allows satan access to his authority to cause havoc on the earth.

Many of these men who yield their authority to satan are really contributing to the power of darkness and coming under its influence.

Satan now empowers different people within that kingdom with hierarchy and rank as it pleases him.

He offered this to Jesus but Jesus refused it completely. He wanted Jesus' authority but he disguised it as giving Jesus something that Jesus did not really need and could do without. No right thinking being wants to be number two in satan's kingdom.

Satan's access into this earth is man.

Treat your body right

Forasmuch then as the children are partakers of flesh and blood, he also himself likewise took part of the same; that through death he might destroy him that had the power of death, that is, the devil;
Hebrews 2:14

Wherefore when he cometh into the world, he saith, Sacrifice and offering thou wouldest not, but a body hast thou prepared me:
Hebrews 10.5

Since God did not transfer to satan the power of darkness and his influence over the earth, God cannot take it back. Man did, therefore only as a flesh and blood man could Jesus combat and destroy the devil. A man started the vicious cycle that introduced death into this earth and it is a man that will end it (Rom. 5:19).

If God could have fixed earth from heaven He would have. The visible dimension can only be fixed from within the visible dimension by one with rights to rule there. It is not the same being that controls both the visible and invisible realms as yet. Thus Jesus needed to be born as a man on this earth in the visible dimension. God operated within very tight parameters. These were the parameters imposed by Adam's authority. God honored the authority that He had transferred to Adam. He interferes on the earth through a man.

Jesus had to come through a woman in order to be Abraham's seed, which qualified him as an Adam. God did not cause a human being to appear out of the ground like He did in making Adam's body. God sent His Word to Mary. Mary heard the Angel's message. This caused faith to come to Mary (Rom. 10:17). Mary's faith then released the power of God to overshadow her womb. The Word of God became a baby inside Mary's womb. Mary supplied the biological material that conferred on Jesus a body through which He could function on this earth as another Adam. Jesus was born spiritually alive with no death in His spirit.

How God anointed Jesus of Nazareth with the Holy Ghost and with power: who went about doing good, and healing all that were oppressed of the devil; for God was with him.
Acts 10:38

God did not stand in heaven, in the invisible dimension, wave some wand and declare all men on earth healed. God had to anoint a man on the earth with His power because though He had the power, He needed man's authority in order for that power to flow through a man in order to produce visible results on the earth. It was Jesus of Nazareth that God anointed. It was not Jesus of heaven. Jesus did not do His first miracle until He was 30 years old. He had always been upright and holy, but it was not until He turned thirty and after John's baptism that the miracles started. This shows that just as is the case with all men, when Jesus was born as a man He was born with no innate powers. This was why He did no miracles until after the Holy Spirit anointed him with power. This power functioned in His life as an anointing which He used to carry out His ministry.

Beloved, believe not every spirit, but try the spirits whether they are of God: because many false prophets are gone out into the world.
1 John 4:1

False prophets have gone out into the world. These false prophets are peddling lies and false philosophies. Spirits are behind these philosophies, which they need men in the world to believe in order for these spirits to gain influence in the world. It does not matter what spirits believe about themselves. What matters is what you believe about them. This is because spirits cannot influence the earth until a man on earth believes them. Spirits feed off the energy of your faith or fear and this releases them to act. Man's choices and beliefs release spiritual power as well as spiritual beings to operate on the earth. Since God is also a spirit, in order for God's will to be manifest on the earth, man must believe God. God is not the one releasing man to act on the earth; it is man releasing God to influence the earth. Our faith releases God's power so that together with God we co-create the visible expression of God's will on the earth. If however man believes the devil, man would be an accomplice in co-creating evil on the earth.

9

COOPERATING WITH GOD

Therefore Eli said unto Samuel, Go, lie down: and it shall be, if he call thee, that thou shalt say, Speak, LORD; for thy servant heareth. So Samuel went and lay down in his place. 10 And the LORD came, and stood, and called as at other times, Samuel, Samuel. Then Samuel answered, Speak; for thy servant heareth.
1 Samuel 3:9-10

Real prayer started at the point Samuel began to respond to God's prompting. God had been speaking to Samuel though Samuel did not know that it was God. God had said as much as He could without Samuel's cooperation. Our aim in prayer is not to get God to speak to us but to enable us to listen to what God has been saying to us. It was Samuel's responsibility to hear God say the things that would bring to pass the plans of God. What we traditionally call prayer involves zero listening. Those who see no need to listen often feel that God is silent. It is when we get quiet enough that we hear Him speak to us.

When Samuel said, "Speak, for thy servant listeneth". Samuel's words supplied the permission for God to speak out in Samuel's hearing what God had purposed to say all along. Samuel's words released power for him to hear and listen to what God was saying. Prayer is our response to God reaching out to us in His Word and within our spirits. The content of our prayer should be the things that God has spoken to us privately as well as generally in His Word. God's Word is pregnant with His power. Real prayer starts with you learning the vocabulary of God as revealed in His Word.

We pray as a means of yielding our authority to God, so that He can bring His will to pass in our world.

God commands you to command

Thus saith the LORD, the Holy One of Israel, and his Maker, Ask me of things to come concerning my sons, and concerning the work of my hands command ye me.
Isaiah 45:11

The works of His hands refer to the things that God wants to bring to pass on earth. God himself has given us a divine responsibility to command. If it were wholly up to God, He would have commanded these things. God commands us because it is not His responsibility to command things. God commands us to command His power. Our command flows from a sense of security based upon God's predictable fatherhood. It is not a sense of superiority over God. We command thus because we know our Father's integrity. It might surprise you, but God commands you to command Him! You are not ordering God around. You are using your commands to release His power.

God's great love commands out of your mouth what is already in His heart to do. When you command as He has instructed, you are acknowledging to be true what He already says is true. It is His Fatherly love that has commanded us to command this way. We know our Father's heart and what is in that heart concerning any issue; therefore we are bold to command manifestations into being! The Fatherhood of God is commanding this of us and we cannot help but command His desire into being. As you fellowship with God's Word, God's desires become your desires. You then command with absolute certainty the desires of your heart.

We are to be so saturated with God's Word and secure in His love that it does not cross our hearts that His answer to us is anything other than an emphatic yes. We are commanding into manifestation what we are persuaded is the desire in His heart for the earth.

For example, Thames Water supply water to my house through the extensive network of pipes criss-crossing England. When I need water I just turn the tap and water flows out. I don't request Thames water to come to my house to turn on the water for me. I don't create the water but it is available for my use whenever I need it. When I turn the tap, I am commanding water to flow out. God wants us to know that He has designed His power to flow in response to our command. He cannot lie. He said it would.

Consider the example of Elijah:

> *Elias was a man subject to like passions as we are, and he prayed earnestly that it might not rain: and it rained not on the earth by the space of three years and six months. And he prayed again, and the heaven gave rain, and the earth brought forth her fruit.*
> *James 5:17-18*

James was teaching the saints about obtaining healing through the power released by the prayer of a righteous man. He cites Elijah drawing down rain as an example of how the principle works. Thus the principles involved in drawing down rain into the earth are the same as those for receiving healing. By tying these two together, James implies that it does not really matter whether we are talking about healing or rainfall, the undergirding principles of power are the same where prayer is concerned.

God is not one way with healing and altogether different concerning everything else. In fact according to the revelation that God gave to James, God was not the one who held back or released rain after forty-two months. That was down to Elijah! Elijah was operating on principles we do well to understand. James compared this to the prayer of faith that saints should pray in getting sick brethren into a clean slate of health. What follows directly is about physical rain but remember that it is the same principle involved in receiving any need met by God's power.

The man side and the Divine side

Let's see what was at the back of Elijah's prayer:

And it came to pass after many days, that the Word of the LORD came to Elijah in the third year, saying, Go, shew thyself unto Ahab; and I will send rain upon the earth.
1 Kings 18:1

We always get the complete picture when we look at the same subject from different angles. Combining the book of kings with James, we see that God was the one that told Elijah that He was sending rain upon the earth. Elijah did not make this up in prayer. The book of Kings focused on God sending the rain while the book of James focused on the part played by Elijah's prayer. This reflects the divine side as well as human side. Taken together, we learn that Elijah's prayer was as important as God "sending" rain. In order to understand how God sends rain, we must remember that God is a spirit being (John 4:24). His realities are spiritual in nature and He acts primarily in the spirit realm. When God said that He would send rain, He would not send it in chemical format as hydrogen and oxygen molecules. He sent it in spiritual form by His Word.

Another thing to note is that though God says to Elijah, "… I will send rain upon the earth", the "earth" in that statement does not refer to the whole world but to the land of Israel (See Jeremiah 22.29). God was speaking to Elijah about the nation of Israel and not the whole earth. Elijah, as a Jew living in Israel, had more authority over the land of Israel than over other parts of the earth.

God wanted to send rain upon the land of Israel but He told Elijah, a man in advance, what He was going to do. Elijah was a man that based his prayer life on God's Word to him. Why did God tell Elijah first? Why did He not just go ahead and saturate that nation with rain? It is because the matter of sending rain upon the land of Israel is not entirely up to God though He wanted that nation to have rain. God looked for a man in Israel that He could tell of His plans to send rain upon Israel. This man then prayed the rain down! Before Elijah prayed, the rain existed in spiritual form as God's promise. Elijah's prayer did not move God to send rain. It was not up to God whether rain fell or not. When Elijah prayed God's Word, he released the power that changed the rain from spiritual form to water form.

God had given Elijah rain in word-form immediately He spoke to him. Thankfully Elijah did not say, "When God sends the rain, I will see rainfall in front of my house. If I don't see rainfall that means He has not sent the rain". That sounds cute but it is veiled unbelief, which uses physical appearances to determine what God is doing or not doing.

First, you hear God say, "Yes"

God needed Elijah as the human agent to transform that rain from word-form to water-form. Elijah was not to get God to say, "Yes". God's Word is His eternal Yes. People who see prayer as a means of getting God to say yes, are standing on the shifty sands of unbelief. First, you hear God say, "Yes", and then you pray.

Elijah triggered the manifestation of the rain in the dimension of time. If that rain had delayed, it would not have been because God changed His mind but because of Elijah's proficiency (or lack of) in hastening the manifestation.

And Elijah said unto Ahab, Get thee up, eat and drink; for there is a sound of abundance of rain.
1 Kings 18:41

The sound of abundant rain was not a physical sound. If it had been so, there would have been no need for Elijah to tell Ahab to prepare for rain. Ahab would have heard the sound and prepared accordingly. Elijah was operating by faith in what God had told him privately. Elijah spoke on earth because he was aware that the raw material for rain was already established in the invisible realm when God spoke.

So Ahab went up to eat and to drink. And Elijah went up to the top of Carmel; and he cast himself down upon the earth, and put his face between his knees, And said to his servant, Go up now, look toward the sea. And he went up, and looked, and said, There is nothing. And he said, Go again seven times. And it came to pass at the seventh time, that

he said, Behold, there ariseth a little cloud out of the sea, like a man's hand. And he said, Go up, say unto Ahab, Prepare thy chariot, and get thee down that the rain stop thee not. And it came to pass in the mean while, that the heaven was black with clouds and wind, and there was a great rain. And Ahab rode, and went to Jezreel.
1 Kings 18:42-45

Elijah was not the Well-if-God-wants-it-to-rain-why-does-He-not-just-send-the-rain-and-get-this-over-with type of saint. Elijah understood that God told him about His plan because God wanted Elijah to do something about it. Elijah responded by praying the rain in. Elijah was a man on the earth releasing the will of God upon the earth. This is the essence of the Lord's Prayer (Mt. 6:10). A man on earth has to speak out the will of God on the earth in order to release the power for its fulfilment. God does not work randomly on the face of the earth. To people like Ahab, the rain falling all happened "suddenly". People who reason that way would conclude that God had somehow decided that enough was enough and had determined that it was time on His mystical calendar to reach out to Israel with rain. The Ahab-type would think that it was all up to God to send rain whenever and wherever He desires on the earth. The will of God came to pass because a man alive on the earth in Ahab's generation was ushering the will of God into the earth through prayer.

If Elijah had not prayed out God's plan and no other man had been willing to do so in Elijah's absence, the drought would have lasted for much longer. That rain would have remained in its spiritual form until a man released it into the earth realm.

God speaks from the spirit realm

For no word from God shall be void of power.
Luke 1:37 (ASV)

Whenever God speaks, His word has power to cause fulfilment. The Word of God is not void of power. God speaks from the spirit realm. He reaches out to men spiritually. These men have both a spiritual as well as a physical component to their being therefore they receive from God spiritually then release into the physical dimension the power contained within the Word of God.

God does not always find Elijahs who will tap into His will and intelligently use their words, prayers and actions to supply the critical mass of human cooperation that releases the power already contained within God's will.

And said to his servant, Go up now, look toward the sea. And he went up, and looked, and said, There is nothing. And he said, Go again seven times.
1 Kings 18:43

Elijah kept telling his servant to go look towards the sea to check for what was happening in the clouds. The servant came back six times saying there was nothing where Elijah expected that there'd be something. Manifestation tends to develop gradually out of the unseen realm into the visible dimension. Elijah could see it with the eye of faith. This gradual build-up suggests that the manifestation of God's will to bring rain did not happen all at once. You can have less or more manifestation (Mk. 4:28). It is not up to God but men operating intelligently upon the earth. How much manifestation we experience is up to us. Elijah's prayer in the present was bridging between the unseen realm where God had spoken in the past and the visible dimension where the rain would fall in the future. God's original Word to Elijah was the raw material for rain; you could say God gave Elijah the rain in word form. Elijah's prayer released the rain into the nation of Israel by turning it from its spiritual word-form into its physical water-form so that others could experience the refreshing of rain.

Elijah's actions in continually sending his servant to look towards the sea leads us to believe that the power of God also operates in discrete quantities, just like physical energy operates in the visible dimension! Elijah's persistence in faith and prayer resulted in the gradual build-up in the clouds. The more Elijah supplied words in prayer, the more of the Word-form-to-water-form transfer was taking place. Those seven times that Elijah went through this operation, he was not pleading with God or convincing God to send rain. God started the whole idea of sending rain in the first place. Prayer is not man coercing God. When Elijah's servant did not see the critical mass of manifestation that Elijah was anticipating, Elijah did more "power transfers" in prayer. Elijah was so developed in this way of operating that it took him having seven tries to cause enough critical mass of rain clouds to appear in the skies over that nation. I don't know how much time passed between God telling Elijah about rain and the arrival of rain clouds. Elijah's persistence was responsible for the appearance of the power as rain clouds, while God's Word was responsible for supplying the power. His prayer transferred that power from its spiritual form into the form that causes water vapour to form rain clouds. Elijah's prayers caused a cloud of possibilities to appear in the sky.

To drive home the points, let's do some thought experiments: When Elijah prayed and sent his servant to check for the manifestation of the rain clouds, and the servant returned saying there was no cloud. Elijah could have taken the servant's response to mean that he had failed. He could have concluded that prayer was a complicated mysterious practice based on chance. In that case he would have doubted that he had the raw material to form the rain clouds. This doubt would have cancelled the effectiveness of his prayer. There would have been no manifestation of rain.

Elijah was convinced that the servant's response was subject to change. Elijah had already received the rain in its spiritual form from God. His act of praying in faith had released the power within God's Word. Once released, that power continues to work. His faith was changing the mighty power within God's Word to physical rain clouds. If he does not doubt, that process will continue and spiritual power will become water molecules that falls as rain on that nation. God's answer was not taking time; it was the full manifestation that was taking time.

When full manifestation takes time, the challenge is that the passage of time itself could tempt Elijah to entertain doubts in his heart concerning the answer that he already had. This doubt would subsequently wage war against the answers that were starting to manifest.

Elijah's act of praying in faith had released the power within God's Word. Once we release the power of God, it continues to work. One reason for delay is that though power is released to change things in the natural, there are other external energies that challenge the manifestation of the answer. Elijah took additional steps that reduced the time it would take for manifestation of rain to come. The servant's initial response painted a picture of clouds without rain. Elijah attacked the image of clouds-without-rain with his persistence in calling the rain into being. His continuous commands were dismantling doubt and preventing it from taking root in his heart. This caused the rain to show up faster. This is the route we should take.

When we pray we are causing the power within the promises of God to transfer from their invisible-word-form to their material equivalent. As we pray, this transfer from spiritual to physical is taking place in discrete quantities. It continues to do so until there is a critical mass of that spiritual substance that manifests in a total experience of our desires.

Why does God not just drop all the manifestation on us all at once in the physical? The short answer is that God would if He could but God doesn't because He has given man charge over the earth. God provides answers spiritually. We engage in concepts like prayer so as to cause the provisions of God to manifest in our physical world.

Ask in the imperative mood

Tremendous power is made available through a good man's earnest prayer. Do you remember Elijah? He was a man like us but he prayed earnestly that it should not rain. In fact, not a drop fell on the land for three and a half years. Then he prayed again, the heavens gave the rain and the earth sprouted with vegetation as usual.
James 5:16-18 (JB Phillips)

Jesus teaches us to ask (in the imperative mood) that God's will be done on earth (Mt 6:10). The will of God is obvious once His nature is known. God's will demonstrates His nature. You can only ask that His Will be done if you know God's nature. When Jesus says "your will be done on earth", He is commanding and not requesting. It is not a question but a command. This is dominion over outcomes in the seen realm. He is not commanding God but things on earth. We are commanding available power to take on the shape of the thing desired. We are acknowledging that God's divine ability is already available as power and our spoken words of command are causing that power to change from word-form into material substance that meets the need.

Elijah was not pleading with God any of those seven times. Elijah's prayer of faith had released the power contained within God's promise and the power continued to work once released by his prayers. His repetition was to overcome any external energy that mounted resistance as well as to release more power. He prayed those seven times to hasten manifestation. Seven represents completeness and perfection. It teaches that we should be vigilant and thorough with our focused prayer.

Jesus repeated the same prayer thrice

He went away again the second time, and prayed, saying, O my Father, if this cup may not pass away from me, except I drink it, thy will be done. And he came and found them asleep again: for their eyes were heavy. And he left them, and went away again, and prayed the third time, saying the same words.
Matthew 26:42-44

In the Garden of Gethsemane Jesus declared, "My soul is exceedingly sorrowful" (Mt. 26:38). His soul did not adjust to sorrow and take it as the norm. The soul is made up of the mind, the will as well as the emotions. When Jesus said that His soul was exceedingly sorrowful, He lets us into a secret. His challenge at that hour was not with the world or the devil but with His own soul. The crushing gravity of the sins of the world was headed His direction. This was a heavy load in deed. He sweated blood! His soul was not fully aligned on the matter at hand. There was discord between his mind, will and emotion. His soul was heavy. His prayer was to transfer power to strengthen His resolve.

The Greek word used for prayer here means the outpouring of the soul. The sheer enormity of the task at hand registered in the mind, will and emotions of Jesus and He struggled in his soul realm. There are things that your mind grasps but your emotions struggles with and is quite unready for. He released tremendous power in prayer to cause His soul to function as a single unit. The task ahead of Him was the redemption of the whole world. His spirit was willing but His flesh was weak.

Jesus prayed the same prayer three times. It was a prayer of commitment to divine will. He was absorbing enough spiritual substance to bring His soul into a place of peace and resoluteness. His human spirit had already locked into the victory but His soul was not yet at the same place of victory that His spirit was in. The calm that He demonstrated throughout all the mocking, various trials and beatings was the product of the peace of God that had gained control of His soul. He prayed until His soul located the peace of God that had always been available from the Father. He had mastery of His soul for the monumental task ahead. He did not act out of character even when the people goaded Him. He had prayed His soul into a complete unity within itself.

God's answer already exists in power form. We receive and command its expression into being through prayer. As we continue to command manifestation, we are mostly dealing with external resistance as well as steadying ourselves so that we can continue to release the power of God through prayer. It was Michelangelo who said, "The statue lies within the stone." In this context, prayer is our sculpting tool to chip away what obstructs the emergence of the perfection within. God gives us the stone while we unveil the statue already existing within the stone.

10

RELEASING
AUTHORITY

*And Jesus said unto the Centurion, Go thy way; and as thou hast
believed, so be it done unto thee. And his servant was healed in the
selfsame hour.*
Matthew 8:13

From Luke's account we know that the Centurion had made a
request to Jesus through the elders (Luke 7:3). Jesus and this
Centurion did not need to meet in person for him to receive
results!

This Centurion was sensitive to the tradition of the Jews (Luke
7:3)

Loved the nation of Israel (Luke 7:5)

Built a synagogue for the Jews (Luke 7:5)

Therefore the Elders felt he was good enough for his servant to be healed (Luke 7:4)

Jesus looked past all that and marveled because of the Centurion's faith (Luke 7:9)

Jesus said the most important thing was what the Centurion believed (Mt 8:13)

People often think they are deserving of divine help because of their character and good works. Others might even take up our cause because our good works motivate people to help us. While good works give a good standing before men, they do not make us receive from God. What counts is what we believe. If that Centurion with all his outstanding morality and good works had believed wrongly, he would have forfeited the mercy of God and cancelled out its effect with wrong thinking and believing.

Your belief links you with omnipotence

It was not the Centurion that was sick. Someone else was going to receive healing based on this Centurion's faith. Jesus told that Centurion, "As thou hast believed, so be it done onto thee". Thus in Jesus' estimation, it mattered what this Centurion actually believed! Jesus did not place the responsibility for healing on God. What the Centurion believed is what would happen. Our praying should be a means of releasing our believing. When you pray be absolutely certain of what you believe. What you believe is what unlocks power for you.

What you believe connects you and yours with an infinite cloud of divine power. Health was going to manifest in that servant within one hour as an outward manifestation of the belief of that Centurion. What if this Centurion had believed that his servant would die of that sickness? Death was already at work in the form of sickness. It would have operated unhindered and that servant would have died prematurely. The Centurion's perception of death would return to him with venom just as he had perceived it. He would have reaped death. This servant will relate towards his master as a healthy man when he gets home primarily because his master's faith anticipates this. What you believe changes you and affects how others will relate towards you. What you believe while praying matters. We use the Word of God to eliminate limiting beliefs and thoughts. We use the words of our mouth in prayer to establish the release of power in line with God's Word.

And when Jesus was entered into Capernaum, there came unto him a Centurion, beseeching him, 6 And saying, Lord, my servant lieth at home sick of the palsy, grievously tormented. And Jesus saith unto him, I will come and heal him. The Centurion answered and said, Lord, I am not worthy that thou shouldest come under my roof: but speak the Word only, and my servant shall be healed. For I am a man under authority, having soldiers under me: and I say to this man, Go, and he goeth; and to another, Come, and he cometh; and to my servant, Do this, and he doeth it. When Jesus heard it, he marvelled, and said to them that followed, Verily I say unto you, I have not found so great faith, no, not in Israel.
Matthew 8:5-10

Jesus and that Centurion did not see each other. Luke stated it factually by showing that they conversed through the elders who were the go-between. Matthew records the meeting of the Centurion and Jesus because he recorded it from spiritual perspective. Matthew shows that, whatever you say, even if it is through others, actually represents you. You and your words are one. When Jesus got close to the house, the Centurion sent friends to tell Jesus not to come to his house (Luke 7:6). He said that all that Jesus needed to do was to speak the Word only and his servant would be healed. This Centurion was highly developed in the power and authority of words. Jesus did not need to get to the Centurion's home for the Centurion's faith did not demand that. The Centurion's faith moved the power resident in Jesus, transported it and emptied it into the body of the servant to drive out sickness and disease! He said that Jesus only needed to speak the Word. Any sound would have been enough to heal that servant. Jesus said what the Centurion said. He told the Centurion that the servant was healed just as the Centurion had spoken (The Centurion spoke what he believed)!

What the Centurion knew

Jesus' encounter with the Centurion establishes a direct connection between authority and faith. They are two sides of the same coin.

The Centurion did not once use the word "faith" or "believe"!

The Centurion understood authority and how to use it. He spoke and reasoned in absolute terms. The soldiers did not act on the Centurion's thoughts. They acted on his will expressed through the words of his mouth. Authority is released whenever you exercise your will. It is transferred through words.

This Centurion was convinced that just as he had military authority and absolute chain of command over his soldiers, so Jesus had authority over sicknesses, the foul works of satan, demonic beings and their operations. He saw Jesus as a higher-ranking official than sickness and disease. He did not anticipate that God would need to do anything. He felt that the disease had not left because its commanding officer, Jesus the Prophet from Nazareth, had not given the diseases their marching orders. He did not factor in the possibility of the diseases staging a mutiny. They were only active in his sick servant's body because Jesus,

the man with authority over sickness, had not released the power
to cause the sickness to leave.

The Centurion's words of authority made a demand on the
power of God resident in Jesus. He knew that the servant did
not need to see Jesus or be touched by Him in order for authority
to work. This was enough to manifest the total healing of his
servant! His words (authority) transferred power from Jesus to
his servant by his faith.

He understood the effectiveness of one-word commands like -
Go! Come!

Jesus does not determine outcomes – your believing does

The Government of Rome had supplied the power to back that
Centurion as commanding officer over 100 soldiers. It was up to
him to use it and boy did he know how to use it! This Centurion
holds the distinction of being the only individual in the Bible
that reversed the suggestion of Jesus and Jesus praised him
for it! Jesus was likely planning to come to the man's house to
exercise authority over the sickness and disease by touching the
servant. The Centurion told Jesus not to bother coming because
authority is released by a command. A man with authority is
more effective when he speaks than by any other means. People
that appreciate authority know the power of faith-filled words.
Through that man's authority, the power of God was transferred
out of the Lord Jesus and operated on his servant elsewhere.
The Centurion did not entertain the idea that a junior ranking
officer (sickness) will refuse to obey. He believed that authority
operates the same way in all dimensions therefore sicknesses had
to go! As a career soldier, the power was in the Government at
Rome but the Centurion used his words to release his authority

over the soldiers under him. In the healing of his servant, the power was resident in Jesus. The faith present in the Centurion's words released the power out of Jesus and transferred it onto the Centurion's servant.

For the believer today, the power is not in Heaven but within our spirits (Eph. 3:20) and it is released through our words flowing from a consciousness of authority.

The Centurion did not anticipate that the Soldiers would only respond to Caesar. Both the Lord Jesus and that Centurion did not expect that the sicknesses would only respond to God. The Lord Jesus had always been capable of staying at one spot and releasing the Word of command to go heal people at any location on the earth during His earth walk. We did not see much of that because Jesus had not met anyone that placed a demand on that dimension of His operation therefore He operated sub-optimally. Jesus operated within the limits of man's cooperation with him. Could this Centurion have told the sickness to leave? What we do know is that he believed Jesus could.

This Centurion told Jesus, "speak the Word only and my servant shall be healed" The Centurion understood that the spoken command of Jesus as the commanding officer was equal to His presence. He believed that the Word of Jesus was as effective as Jesus himself and was the equivalent of Jesus himself standing inside that house at the servant's bedside reversing the process of death. Jesus was positively amazed at the audacity of the Centurion's thinking. He did not correct the Centurion's perspective. That Centurion was bang on point!

Authority is in degrees

The word "Centurion" implies scope. The Centurion is an officer who has command of one hundred soldiers. This Centurion would not have authority over the whole army. He has authority where he had control. If he believed that he had no control, then irrespective of his rank, he would not be able to reap maximum benefit from his authority. The Centurion knew the limitations, scope and boundary of his authority. Within the bounds of his authority, he had absolute chain of command. There are areas of life where others have authority over and we need to recognize their authority in order for us to get maximum benefit. Authority is in degrees. I cannot command someone else's job to become mine because I am the king's kid. If I did, that would not be authority but covetousness wrapped in spiritual sounding jargon! Faith will not claim that some other person's job or position is yours in Jesus' name or any name for that matter!
Jesus called the Centurion's declaration of authority great faith. Great faith understands what it can and cannot do as well as the scope of its operations. Whatever you have been given control over, you can exercise authority in that area. God did not give Adam dominion over other human beings, so it is impossible to say that you are taking authority over the human will. Anyone who tries to do this is being manipulative.

Authority and faith are twins

The Centurion was operating from an understanding of authority, yet Jesus commended him for great faith. A person who understands authority will be operating in faith. By extension, a person who understands faith would have to walk in their authority. Authority and faith operate by the same principles. They are both released by spoken words of command that demand immediate action. A man of authority understands that we can tell things to go. We can also command them to come. We command the mountains and hindrances to go! Then we command our desires to come! (Mk. 11:23-24)

Faith is a spiritual substance

Now faith is the substance of things hoped for, the evidence of things not seen.
Hebrews 11:1

You cannot develop your faith except you understand what faith is as a concept. Bible faith is much more than believing in the existence of God. Demons actually believe that God exists but that does not qualify as Bible faith (James 2:19). Bible faith is a spiritual substance that is the evidence of the unseen. That term "things not seen" describes things in the unseen eternal dimension. Unseen things are the building blocks of the eternal realm. Faith is the substance of the "not seen" realm. Faith is the substance or building block of the spirit realm. What atoms are to the natural realm, faith is to the spirit realm. Faith is a substance having to do with things "not seen". These things "not seen" were used to build out the visible realm (Heb. 11:3). Therefore, the fundamental material that God works with is faith.

Let's see how faith turns resurrection power into salvation in those who received eternal life and got born again in the Bible.

Consider Lydia, who was Paul's first convert in Europe.

And on the sabbath we went out of the city by a river side, where prayer was wont to be made; and we sat down, and spake unto the women which resorted thither. And a certain woman named Lydia, a seller of purple, of the city of Thyatira, which worshipped God, heard us: whose heart the

Lord opened, that she attended unto the things which were spoken of Paul.
Acts 16:13-14

As a Jew, Lydia worshipped God in a Jewish way before she was exposed to the ministry of Paul. She was not yet born again. She had as much need of eternal life as any Gentile though she was a Jew. It is implied that Lydia was the only one in that group by the riverside that received eternal life. God has already provided salvation therefore we can pray that people's heart be opened to receive the Gospel.

All her prayers at the riverside could not magically get her saved. She needed to hear God's Word with an open heart. The Lord opened her heart so that she could attend to what Paul was saying. There was something pivotal about what Paul was saying. God opens people's heart in order that they might focus it on the Word. Without the Word, an open heart will as readily drink in spiritual junk. God has limited His saving power to what the preacher will preach from God's Word as well as the degree of attention the hearer will give to the spoken Word of God. Lydia had been praying but she needed to attend to God's Word. Prayer should help focus your attention on the Word. It is only as we stay attentive to the Word, that prayer achieves its intended purpose. It is scriptural to pray that God will open someone's heart but only do so if you know they will be exposed to the truth of God's Word.

It was still up to Lydia to attend to what Paul was speaking. When we attend to the Word it plants the Word in our heart.

Resurrection power released by preaching

For Christ sent me not to baptize, but to preach the gospel: not with wisdom of words, lest the cross of Christ should be made of none effect.

For the preaching of the cross is to them that perish foolishness; but unto us which are saved it is the power of God.
1 Corinthians 1:17-18

The cross of Christ is not the piece of wood on Golgotha. That term is a shorthand way of talking about all the work that Christ did in redemption. God has already generated enormous power to meet all our needs through the cross of Christ. "The cross" was God in action. Today, man needs to respond to God's move. We don't need to get God to move again. There is no need that will come up in your life that God has not already supplied power to meet though the cross of Christ.

As enormous as it is, the power generated at the cross can be rendered ineffective.

God stores the power in His Word. We transport that power by the preaching of the cross. When we preach the Word, we are transporting the enormous power in the cross to the hearer.

The reason why the cross is ineffectual in some people is because the gospel is not preached. People hear a lot that is termed "preaching" but it is not the gospel therefore, no power is transported to them. Prayer alone never really got anyone born again. Prayer alone cannot save the world. Jesus has already provided saving power through His resurrection. We get that power to those who need salvation by preaching it. Praying for someone who will not be exposed to the Word of God is ineffective.

For after that in the wisdom of God the world by wisdom knew not God, it pleased God by the foolishness of preaching to save them that believe.
1 Corinthians 1:21

When we ask God to save someone, what are we really asking for? God cannot send Jesus back to the cross! There is no need asking Him to save anyone today. He has already supplied saving power through the Cross of Christ. Someone must do the preaching for it is by the foolishness of preaching that God works today. The saving power is locked within the message itself. It is transported through preaching to the hearers. Then that power is released inside the heart of those that believe. When we believe, God does not send Jesus to the cross again. Our believing releases the power of what Jesus had accomplished into our lives so that it becomes our experience.

We are not praying to God to give salvation. God already provided salvation because He loved us and not because we prayed for it (John 3:16). It is already given and God cannot "un-give" it. We want the sinner to receive salvation. We can pray to cancel the things hindering him from believing (2 Cor. 4:3-4). We can pray about the filters and mindset preventing him from hearing the good news. We can pray that people with the gospel will preach to him (Mt. 9:38). We do not ask God to save the sinner (Rom. 5:8).

Deposit the substance of God's Word into the heart

We need a means of releasing the power already contained within the Word. This is why we preach. Preaching unleashes the power contained within the resurrection of Jesus (1 Cor. 1:18). The substance of God's Word is transferred through the ear into the heart of the hearer. This Word contains God's faith (Rom. 10:17). As our preaching is heard, we are planting God's faith into the heart of the hearer of the gospel (Mk. 4:20). As we preach God's Word, we are transporting more of this substance for the ear of the hearers to feed into their own heart.

All that spiritual substance in the heart does not benefit the hearer until the hearer believes and then starts voicing the Word of God (Rom 1:16). It is this process of voicing what you believe that releases the saving power already contained within the spiritual substance of God's Word (Rom 10:10). It is at this stage that the spirit of the sinner gets recreated. The power was in the cross. God stored it within His Word. We transported it by preaching. It enters the human heart through hearing. The hearer then believes what is heard. When we speak what we believe, we release the tremendous power, which was generated at the cross of Christ.

Salvation is the greatest miracle that happens to a man. Since this is the method of delivery of salvation to men, you can rest assured that this is the way God works on earth today. The rest of our Christian walk follows that same pattern of faith that we used to receive salvation (Col. 2:6). Change happens when the voice of faith releases enough spiritual substance of God's Word until there is a critical mass, which the Holy Spirit uses to recreate our human spirit.

You can be the preacher as well as the hearer

We are familiar with this principle of transporting saving power through preaching to another who needed God's power for salvation. However it does not only work if it is between the preacher and another person who is the hearer. It will work once there is a preacher and one who hears what the preacher is saying. The preacher and the hearer can be the same person. The Word of God in its spiritual form is spiritual substance (John 6:63). We speak it in order to transfer it from where it is stored. We hear it in order to transfer it to where it is needed in our heart. We then believe and speak to release its power from our heart into any area where we need God's help manifested.

Visible and invisible things

While we look not at the things which are seen, but at the things which are
not seen: for the things which are seen are temporal; but the things which
are not seen are eternal.
2 Corinthians 4:18

In God's creation, at least as far as we can tell, there are two
kinds of things. There are the things that are the building block
of the temporal realm and there are other things that belong
in the invisible realm. The things that belong to the invisible
realm are called "things not seen". We must not assume that
just because they are not seen they are unreal. That phrase "not
seen" speaks of things beyond the spectrum of what our five
senses accept as reality. It describes reality beyond the physical
realm. The things that are referred to as things "seen" will change
no matter how permanent they look, but the things "not seen"
persist and remain unchanged. The "not seen" realm refers to
the spirit dimension. This is the eternal dimension.

Through faith we understand that the worlds were framed by the Word
of God, so that things which are seen were not made of things which do
appear.
Hebrews 11:3

When we strip everything to the basics, we find that the things
which are seen are not made up of visible things. They are made
up of unseen things. This means that unseen things make up
well over 99% of the fabric of all reality. What our biological
senses know as reality is a minute portion of a fraction of a tiny
speck of the unseen realm. That puts everything in perspective.

The Greek word translated "world" in that verse is not the one
you'd use for planets. It does not even necessarily refer to the
earth in that verse. The Greek word used refers to arrangements

and order. Whenever God wants to establish order, He says something. These spoken words change the substance of faith into visible things. Spoken words are a means of changing invisible things into visible form. There is an infinite supply of invisible things. The only scarcity is that of visible things. God's Word contains eternal power. Faith is the substance of unseen things. When we speak God's word, faith comes. This means spiritual substance comes. At the same time, those words supply energy. The power changes the invisible substance into whatever answers we need manifested in visible form.

God used the words of His mouth, which is a supply of infinite energy, to frame faith, which is the substance of things. God used things that are "not visible" or things "not seen" to build out things that are "seen". God did not use visible things to bring forth the visible universe. The seen realm, which consists of what our senses feel and touch, is actually a by-product of the things of the unseen realm. The sound of God's Word released the faith substance that changed form to become our material universe. This is the way it also works for us. Our words are carriers of faith. They will equally be containers of fear substances. When you are speaking God's Word you are releasing packets of energy from God's infinite supply. You can use the words of your mouth to feed the cells of your body with vibrations that become health. Sickness is your body vibrating out of sync with God's power. You can use the words of your mouth charged with the substance of health from God's Word to feed your body with packets of health until the whole is charged with immunity and life power.

*By the Word of the LORD were the heavens made; and all the host
of them by the breath of his mouth. He gathereth the waters of the sea
together as an heap: he layeth up the depth in storehouses. Let all the earth
fear the LORD: let all the inhabitants of the world stand in awe of him.
For he spake, and it was done; he commanded, and it stood fast.*
Psalm 33:6,9

God's starting point was not nothingness but faith. He used His words as the bridge between the things "seen" and the things "not seen". This is the way faith works. When God spoke in the beginning, the unseen substance of faith changed form and caused the things that became the earth to stand fast. This is how the earth came to be in the first place. Everything that we see out there in the vastness of space is made up of the spiritual substance of faith. This is why they stand fast. The faith of God holds this universe together. If you want the substance of faith to cause things to stand fast in your world, you need to start hearing yourself speak God's Word.

You are to speak God's Word, so that by hearing God's Word, you cause the substance of things "not seen" to begin to flow into your world and build out new order and arrangements. Whenever we speak words, whether as a confession or as prayer, it is this fundamental principle that we are tapping into. God is not the one that needs to speak His word today; that is your responsibility. Think of your words as the highway on which you transport the spiritual material, which brings manifestation into your world.

Every born again one has the God kind of faith, the raw material of the invisible realm, within their spirits. It is as we begin to hear ourselves speak God's Word that this faith material flows out of our spiritual nature into our heart and from our heart into our circumstance in order to manifest the will of God.

Faith's rebuke

The primary way that Jesus exercised His faith was by rebuking things. We must learn how to use our faith this way also.

And when Jesus was entered into Capernaum, there came unto him a

Centurion, beseeching him, And saying, Lord, my servant lieth at home
sick of the palsy, grievously tormented. And Jesus saith unto him, I will
come and heal him. The Centurion answered and said, Lord, I am not
worthy that thou shouldest come under my roof: but speak the Word
only, and my servant shall be healed. For I am a man under authority,
having soldiers under me: and I say to this man, Go, and he goeth; and to
another, Come, and he cometh; and to my servant, Do this, and he doeth
it. When Jesus heard it, he marvelled, and said to them that followed,
Verily I say unto you, I have not found so great faith, no, not in Israel.
Matthew 8:5-10

This Centurion is not like most Christians, who would believe
that they are taking authority over sicknesses and diseases by
saying, "I take authority over you in Jesus name". He does not
say to the lower ranking soldiers under his command, "I take
authority over you".

He says to them, "Go!" or "Come!"

Saying, "I take authority over you" is as powerful as saying, "the
moon is smaller than the sun". It is informational but does not
demand any action or cause any change!

And Jesus rebuked him, saying, Hold thy peace, and come out of him.
And when the devil had thrown him in the midst, he came out of him,
and hurt him not.
Luke 4:35

Greek scholars tell us that the Greek word translated "rebuke"
actually means to deliver judgment from a higher standard. The
higher standard is the position of absolute dominion over the
works of satan because of the resurrection of Jesus. Every born
again one possesses this higher standard. We are higher ranking
officials than the devil or any of his demons.

As you study the Gospels you discover that Jesus did not really spend time praying for the sick or concerning sickness. He rebuked things a lot, especially sickness. Jesus rebuked by saying. Jesus consistently used the power of rebuke to deal with things. Jesus did not rebuke the demon by saying, "I rebuke thee", but by saying, "Hold thy peace and come out of him". You deliver a scriptural rebuke through spoken words. In all instances where Jesus rebuked, He did not leave it in the thought realm. You are not as effective releasing a rebuke through your thoughts as you'll be using your words. Our words deliver authority in ways that thoughts cannot.

Jesus definitely rebuked the wind, but not by saying, "Wind, I rebuke you".

And he arose, and rebuked the wind, and said unto the sea, Peace, be still. And the wind ceased, and there was a great calm.
Mark 4:39

Jesus brought about a great calm by first rebuking the wind and then by speaking peace to the sea. Note that order. He rebuked the hindrance after which He spoke His desire (Mk. 11:23-24).

And he saith unto them, Why are ye fearful, O ye of little faith? Then he arose, and rebuked the winds and the sea; and there was a great calm. But the men marvelled, saying, What manner of man is this, that even the winds and the sea obey him!
Matthew 8:26-27

Jesus was the manifestation of God's righteousness. He knew that these troublesome winds were not because of personal sin in His life. People who are not established in righteousness condemn themselves whenever things go wrong. They think it must mean that they have sinned. The troublesome sea was the adverse effect of living in a fallen world groaning under the effects of Adam's sin.

We have no record of what He actually said to the winds but there are other places where He rebuked things, so we can work out what He said. The words or rebuke released the power that caused the winds to cease. The disciples could not see that God intended that their own words should release power too. Jesus had conversations with the winds and the sea. We should too. Fear caused them to ignore the faith that they had. Therefore, power did not manifest to drive out the storm. Their fear caused them to operate in little faith.

Now when the sun was setting, all they that had any sick with divers diseases brought them unto him; and he laid his hands on every one of them, and healed them. 41 And devils also came out of many, crying out, and saying, Thou art Christ the Son of God. And he rebuking them suffered them not to speak: for they knew that he was Christ.
Luke 4:40, 41

Jesus rebuked demons.

And he stood over her, and rebuked the fever; and it left her: and immediately she arose and ministered unto them.
Luke 4:39

This fever was not psychological. It actually left. While we expect demons to hear and respond to a rebuke, we are not quite ready for sicknesses and the storms of life to also hear what we say in our rebuke. Jesus rebuked fever just like He rebuked demons, the sea and the wind and the fever left her. Anything that comes against us, whether they are the direct activity of demons or the effects of living in a fallen world have the ability to hear us and respond to the power released through our command.

And Jesus rebuked him, saying, Hold thy peace, and come out of him.
Mark 1:25

Biblical rebuke is commanding because you know that you have authority. It is directional and not just a threat to do something. When a person says, "I rebuke you satan", they are threatening to rebuke the devil. Threatening to rebuke is not the same thing as actually rebuking. In this instance, the rebuke that Jesus spoke to the demon was, "Be silent, and come out of him!"

You can reduce it to – Silence! Out!

Now, that's scriptural rebuke.

In order to know if you have rebuked scripturally, go through this thought experiment in your own mind:

What have I said?

What do I mean?

Have I said what I really want done?

Who have I asked to do it?

If this was spoken to me, would I be clear about the outcomes?

The Centurion in Matthew 8 does not say to the soldier, "I want you to do something for me". He simply releases the command and that command becomes the soldier's commission.

You will find that people that rebuke by saying, "I rebuke you", are also the type that will bless by saying, "I bless you". However, the way God blesses is not by saying, "I bless you".

And God blessed them, saying, Be fruitful, and multiply, and fill the
waters in the seas, and let fowl multiply in the earth
Genesis 1:22

Notice how God blessed the animal creation. God's blessing does not even include the word "bless". He blessed them by saying. You deliver a scriptural blessing through words. The blessing is what is spoken, "be fruitful and multiply ...". Too many times we threaten to bless others without really blessing them.

And God blessed them, and God said unto them, Be fruitful, and
multiply, and replenish the earth, and subdue it: and have dominion over
the fish of the sea, and over the fowl of the air, and over every living thing
that moveth upon the earth.
Genesis 1:28

Again, notice that God blessed Adam and Eve by saying, "Be fruitful and multiply". Those words contained the substance of God's blessing. You deliver a scriptural blessing through spoken words.

Creation is in convulsions

For the earnest expectation of the creature waiteth for the manifestation of
the sons of God. For the creature was made subject to vanity, not willingly,
but by reason of him who hath subjected the same in hope, Because the
creature itself also shall be delivered from the bondage of corruption into
the glorious liberty of the children of God.
Romans 8:19-21

Adam introduced sin into this earth and sin let in death (Rom. 5:12). The penalty was death and not loss of authority (Gen. 2:17). It is nowhere stated that because of Adam's sin God withdrew man's mandate to rule and reign. God has never withdrawn from man the mandate to rule this planet. We live in a fallen world. If we do not learn to rebuke the effects of living in a fallen world we will find ourselves at the receiving end of random evil activity that cripples us.

Speak to things

Jesus was a man of prayer. As He prayed, He became more conscious of God's power resident within Him. Through His words, He commanded the power of God. In the Gospels we find that Jesus dealt with more situations in public by saying than He did by praying. His pattern was to pray to God at night and then speak to things for the rest of the day. Jesus spoke to inanimate things and they obeyed Him. He was releasing God's power through words. Jesus practiced a lifestyle that allowed Him to speak to storms. He did not pray about storms. At the tomb of Lazarus, Jesus thanked the Father for hearing Him but then speaks to Lazarus to come forth (John 11:42-43). Jesus rarely prayed for people publicly. When He was ministering to people He spoke to them. We must learn the power of our spoken words.

And he arose, and rebuked the wind, and said unto the sea, Peace, be still.
And the wind ceased, and there was a great calm.
Mark 4:39

In the book of beginnings (Genesis), we do not find God saying, "Let there be storms and Tsunamis". Storms, tsunamis and tragedy are not God's design. Adam's transgression turned God's blessings into a curse. This curse is causing havoc in creation. Rivers and seas were not designed to drown people (Gen. 1:10). The characteristic that kills is there today but God did not put it there. The storm did not happen on that sea that night because that was the most sinful spot on the earth at that instant. Jesus said that the evil does not strike at the most sinful places on earth (Lk. 13:4). Evil is not consistent. It is random in its expression. This is the nature of evil.

Jesus understood the nature of God and from that understanding He had a grasp of God's will. God's will and God's nature are one and the same thing. He knew that the storm was contrary to God's nature and that it did not demonstrate the goodness of God. Therefore, instead of succumbing to fear, He commanded the expression of God's will by rebuking the storm. If Jesus had believed that the storm was God-sent to signify His sinfulness, He would have reaped destruction through wrong thinking and believing. Jesus never submitted himself to any storm. He always acted to end it. I am convinced that if Jesus were alive in our day, He would have done to the tsunamis exactly what He did to the storms in His day. You will also find that Jesus did not use the storms of His day as a prophetic commentary on the nearness of the end of days. Today, Christians see the devastation of floods, monsoons and tsunamis which wipe out whole neighborhoods and the first response is to inform everyone that cares to listen that these disasters are the signs of the end, a sort of warning system from God by which we mark our prophetic calendars.

Tsunamis have no regard for anyone. Storms rose up against Jesus in the days of His earth walk. He did not attribute it to His own personal sins or the sins of the people on the boat with Him. He did not interpret them as prophetic signs from His Father. Jesus stopped storms wherever He saw them. Jesus demonstrated that God was not behind the storms by always stopping them when they showed up. Some people have been trained to draw comfort from it but one of the most ugly things to say to a person who has been through a tsunami or similar events is to say, "God is in control and all is OK for God's plan is coming to pass". This is not only impotent theology it is silly. That kind of toxic religious thinking reduces God to someone who loves the limelight so much that He will resort to doing anything in order to grab the headlines and stay relevant. It portrays God as offering succor for the very damages that He has caused. That's not what God is like. He is good, always good and only good.

11

ASKING &
RECEIVING

If you knew who

There cometh a woman of Samaria to draw water: Jesus saith unto her,
Give me to drink. (For his disciples were gone away unto the city to buy
meat.)Then saith the woman of Samaria unto him, How is it that thou,
being a Jew, askest drink of me, which am a woman of Samaria? for the
Jews have no dealings with the Samaritans.Jesus answered and said unto
her, If thou knewest the gift of God, and who it is that saith to thee, Give
me to drink; thou wouldest have asked of him, and he would have given
thee living water.
John 4:7-10

Once this woman had a glimpse of who Jesus was, she would
rise above her bigotry and ask Him to give her drink. Her
asking was controlled by her awareness of the nature of who
it was that she was in concert with. Our prayer changes, as we

know Him. When we know Him, we ask what He wants done and He gets the audience for its performance. She'd ask for drink and He would give because she asked from correctly discerning Him. He did not entertain the possibility of her asking and His not giving.

He already said Yes

Hitherto have ye asked nothing in my name: ask, and ye shall receive, that your joy may be full.
John 16:24

And all things, whatsoever ye shall ask in prayer, believing, ye shall receive.
Matthew 21:22

If ye abide in me, and my words abide in you, ye shall ask what ye will, and it shall be done unto you.
John 15:7

If ye then, being evil, know how to give good gifts unto your children, how much more shall your Father which is in heaven give good things to them that ask him?
Matthew 7:11

Be not ye therefore like unto them: for your Father knoweth what things ye have need of, before ye ask him.
Matthew 6:8

We are to ask according to the Word abiding in us. The Word of God renews our minds and becomes our will. We then ask what we will and it shall be done unto us. This way God guarantees that we will not pray unscriptural prayers. We will be full of the abiding Word; therefore, we would be praying the Word. What we will and what God wills are exactly one.

In prayer, we must remember the fact that our Father God is primarily a giver and not a withholder. We are also to know the good things that He has given so that when we ask, we ask knowing that the giving is already guaranteed. In other words, we are to pray because we know that God has already said "yes". Thus prayer is not to get God's yes. When we pray, we are saying "yes" just as God has already said yes, in order for that "yes" to become someone's experience on the earth.

Why ask?

Ye lust, and have not: ye kill, and desire to have, and cannot obtain: ye
fight and war, yet ye have not, because ye ask not.
James 4:2

James says "Ye have not because ye ask not".

Our prayers and our Word content are connected. Let the Word build you into a strong person of prayer. A person of the Word should also be a person of prayer. Not only are we limited by our prayer life; God is also limited by our prayer life. What God wants manifested is vastly different from what ends up getting executed in the earth because of the variable imposed by man's willingness to cooperate with the will of God in prayer. We have a divine invitation to ask. It appears that we never quite get to the place of asking at the depth and level that we should be asking at. There are things that God wants done but He has limited Himself to bringing it to pass in cooperation with our asking. God has established what His ability can bring to pass. Our asking releases His ability on our behalf.

Through prayer, we are making ourselves a part of His love

program. We are not enlisting Him into ours or persuading Him to see the rightness of our plea.

> *Ask, and it shall be given you; seek, and ye shall find; knock, and it shall be opened unto you: For every one that asketh receiveth; and he that seeketh findeth; and to him that knocketh it shall be opened.*
> Matthew 7:7-8

Jesus did not even say that those who asked had to be morally perfect. He simply stated that everyone that asks receives. Experience screams loudly that this cannot be the case. We are sure that not everyone that asks receives. We think that we can cite examples. Jesus is correct. We are the ones needing to revise our understanding of what it means to ask as well as receive. When our western mind-set comes across a word like "ask", we immediately impose on it a meaning in line with how we use the word today. We think that to ask means to make a cultured request that might or might not be granted. However, if that is the manner of our asking, we are simply trying to spiritualise uncertainty. The Bible calls this unbelief. Jesus teaches a type of asking which has a guaranteed outcome. A receiving immediately follows His type of asking.

Though God has already provided all things in Christ, His nature does not permit Him to cram these down our throats. God is not that type of being. Our asking is a means of stating our will. When we do not know how to ask, we limit our ability to receive manifestation of that which God has already supplied.

There are five words in the New Testament Greek that usually translate into the English word "ask". When teaching us to "ask" in His name, the Greek word that the Lord Jesus consistently uses is "aiteo", which is a demand of something due (John 15:7,16, John 14:13, John 16:24). It is not an inquiry. Asking is not even about being polite or nice. It means directives released because of understood outcomes. Asking is more than just talking to God. It is a directive, a command. It is like asking a question whose answer you already know. If you knew that God had answered before you called out to Him or even before you finish your sentences, would you speak differently? That is the intent of the word "ask". God illustrated this truth to Isaiah in the following words, "It shall come to pass that before they call, I will answer; and while they are yet speaking, I will hear" (Isaiah 65:24).

We ask because we know that God has pre-approved with a Yes (2 Cor. 1:20)! When we ask, God supplies the answer and we do the receiving.

Jesus answered and said unto them, Verily I say unto you, If ye have faith, and doubt not, ye shall not only do this which is done to the fig tree, but also if ye shall say unto this mountain, Be thou removed, and be thou cast into the sea; it shall be done. And all things, whatsoever ye shall ask in prayer, believing, ye shall receive
Matthew 21:21-22

We are to speak to the problem knowing that we are authorised to do so. Jesus is illustrating what it means to ask. We don't ask God to speak to the mountain. We command the mountain to move because we know we are authorised to do so. In prayer, we speak to God and when we ask in prayer we issue commands to the hindrance that stands in our way.

And when the time of the fruit drew near, he sent his servants to the husbandmen, that they might receive the fruits of it.
Matthew 21:34

When the farmer goes out to pick his crop, he is receiving his harvest. Receiving means you are taking something. You are not sitting back waiting and doing nothing. When you ask biblically you are commanding and releasing directives. When you receive you take.

What it means to Receive

Then Peter said, Silver and gold have I none; but such as I have give I thee: In the name of Jesus Christ of Nazareth rise up and walk. And he took him by the right hand, and lifted him up: and immediately his feet and ankle bones received strength.
Acts 3:6-7

It was as this man stood up that he received strength in his legs. His standing up was his way of receiving strength in his ankle bones. We are not told that it was at that moment that God gave him strength. His action of letting himself be held up completed the action of the power of God. His standing was his way of asking. The consequence was that he received strength in his ankle bones.

Here's another example that illustrates what it means to receive.

Therefore said they unto him, How were thine eyes opened? He answered and said, A man that is called Jesus made clay, and anointed mine eyes, and said unto me, Go to the pool of Siloam, and wash: and I went and washed, and I received sight.
John 9:10-11

Jesus had transferred the power of God onto the man's eyes but that did not open his eyes. This is because God's power is a spiritual substance. The man did not supply any act of faith to release its physical effect. After hands were laid on him, the man walked to the pool blind. It was as he washed that he received his sight. This shows that receiving is not passive. Receiving is a corresponding act of faith. The principles are as follows:

First of all, faith comes by hearing God's Word. We then release faith through spoken words. Manifestation then follows as we act on what we have spoken out of our mouths.

It was as this blind man walked to the pool that he demonstrated the faith that released the anointing, which Jesus had placed upon his eyes. The man received his eyes opened by walking and washing his eyes in the pool. By walking and washing, he was receiving.

The key thing to note is that God does not give us the physical substance (2 Pet 1:3). As believers, God's Spirit releases the spiritual substance of His power into our inner man. Our corresponding action to faith then transforms this spiritual power into a physical manifestation. Our actions of faith bring about the natural results.

Daniel's Example

Through the prophet Jeremiah He said the following regarding Israel's captivity:

> To fulfil the Word of the LORD by the mouth of Jeremiah, until the land had enjoyed her sabbaths: for as long as she lay desolate she kept sabbath, to fulfil threescore and ten years.
> 2 Chronicles 36:21

> For thus saith the LORD, That after seventy years be accomplished at Babylon I will visit you, and perform my good word toward you, in causing you to return to this place.
> Jeremiah 29:10

The prophetic Word concerning Israel's captivity is not in the same category as the Word to Noah that never again will a flood wipe out the whole world (See Genesis 9:11). What God spoke to Noah did not require Noah (or any other human being for that matter) to do anything but hear it. Daniel discovered that the Word of prophecy concerning Israel's captivity required that someone do something about it.

Pray the Word of God

In the first year of Darius the son of Ahasuerus, of the seed of the Medes, which was made king over the realm of the Chaldeans; In the first year of his reign I Daniel understood by books the number of the years, whereof the Word of the LORD came to Jeremiah the prophet, that he would accomplish seventy years in the desolations of Jerusalem. And whiles I was speaking, and praying, and confessing my sin and the sin of my people Israel, and presenting my supplication before the LORD my God for the holy mountain of my God; Yea, whiles I was speaking in prayer, even the man Gabriel, whom I had seen in the vision at the beginning, being caused to fly swiftly, touched me about the time of the evening oblation. And he informed me, and talked with me, and said, O Daniel, I am now come forth to give thee skill and understanding. At the beginning of thy supplications the commandment came forth, and I am come to shew thee; for thou art greatly beloved: therefore understand the matter, and consider the vision.
Daniel 9:1-2, 20-23

Daniel's prayer life drew its power from the understanding that he gained from God's prophetic word.

God had previously supplied a promise of deliverance through Jeremiah the prophet who had prophesied in advance that Israel would be in a seventy-year captivity. Every Word of God contains the power of fulfilment. When God gave this prophetic Word to Jeremiah, He had supplied in advance through that Word, the power to set Israel free from captivity.

Prophet Daniel lived in the midst of the captivity with a lot of other Jews. It appeared to Daniel that Jeremiah's powerful and inspired prophecy of hope and deliverance was unfulfilled. That prophecy was a statement of God's will but just because the will of God is stated, does not in of itself bring that will to pass on the earth. This was because there was no human agent who would recognise that God's part was complete in the unseen realm of the spirit.

The next phase was to be carried out by a man who recognised his authority on the earth. Such a man would take the substance of that prophetic word and ponder on it, in order to plant the faith contained within it into his own heart. He would then act in faith to release the tremendous power of deliverance contained within God's promise! The faith-acts would transform the promise from spiritual substance into physical reality of deliverance from captivity. Until Daniel's intervention, the deliverance existed in the unseen dimension in word-form, awaiting the man who would transform it into material deliverance in the natural realm.

The first step in reversing that captivity was Daniel's discovery of God's promises, which had been spoken out in prophecy form through Jeremiah. This became the seed of God's Word, which Jeremiah planted into his own heart by continuing to hear that prophetic word. He then prayed over the seed of that prophecy to release the power contained within it.

Daniel knew from understanding scriptures that Israel's captivity at that point in time did not reflect the will of God. It was God's will that Israel's captivity be ended. There is a world of difference when it is the Word that ushers you into prayer. The prophecy of Jeremiah was God's answer to the captivity of Israel. By making the prophecy of Jeremiah the content of his prayer, Daniel was praying the answer and not the problem. Daniel shows us that true spirituality does not pray the "issue" at hand but the answer, which is the Word of God. Daniel prayed the will of God into manifestation. Find out what God wants done, then use prayer to usher in the expression of God's plan. Prayer is using God's Word to converse with God. In God's Word, we find what to pray as well as how to pray. The Word of God teaches us to pray. Though prayer comes to man quite naturally, praying scripturally is taught, not just caught out of thin air.

Praying in the correct mood

O my God, incline thine ear, and hear; open thine eyes, and behold our desolations, and the city which is called by thy name: for we do not present our supplications before thee for our righteousnesses, but for thy great mercies. O Lord, hear; O Lord, forgive; O Lord, hearken and do; defer not, for thine own sake, O my God: for thy city and thy people are called by thy name.
Daniel 9:18-19

Now read the same passage in the NIV translation:

"Give ear, our God, and hear; open your eyes and see the desolation of the city that bears your Name. We do not make requests of you because we are righteous, but because of your great mercy. Lord, listen! Lord, forgive! Lord, hear and act! For your sake, my God, do not delay, because your city and your people bear your Name."
Daniel 9:18-19 NIV

Experts at Hebrew grammar tell us that Daniel is praying in the imperative voice. The understanding he had gained from meditating on Jeremiah's prophecy erased any uncertainties in Daniel's heart. The NIV catches the imperative mood best by following his statements with exclamations. When you are full of the Word, your mood in requesting is one where you are commanding manifestations to come forth His words are commanding the release of the power within the prophetic promise. This is what it means to make a request. He is commanding the manifestation of a promise that God had given through the mouth of Prophet Jeremiah.

God had transferred His power into the earth through the prophecy of Prophet Jeremiah. This power remained stored in written form until a man came along who planted it in his heart. By hearing the Word, Daniel was planting the faith of God within his heart (Rom. 10:17). Daniel then released the power contained within the implanted word by his prayer in the imperative mood. This set in motion the process for receiving the manifestation of deliverance from captivity.

God answers speedily

Yea, whiles I was speaking in prayer, even the man Gabriel, whom I had seen in the vision at the beginning, being caused to fly swiftly, touched me about the time of the evening oblation. And he informed me, and talked with me, and said, O Daniel, I am now come forth to give thee skill and understanding. At the beginning of thy supplications the commandment came forth, and I am come to shew thee; for thou art greatly beloved: therefore understand the matter, and consider the vision.
Daniel 9:21-23

"He stood before me and said, 'Daniel, I have come to make things plain to you. You had no sooner started your prayer when the answer was given.
Daniel 9:22 (The Message)

Angel Gabriel revealed to Daniel that as soon as Daniel began to pray the answer was given. Gabriel had come to tell Daniel that God had already answered the prayer though Daniel was still in captivity. This angel was not lying. The captivity continued though the prayer had been answered!

God is a spirit. He gives spiritually. God's answers are spiritual in nature. God gives answers in the spiritual dimension. He does not give physical answers. God first gave the answer in spiritual form to an angel. Later that angel transported the answer to Daniel. This got to Daniel some minutes after the answer had been given originally in the spiritual form.

Daniel was unaware that God had answered the prayer from the minute he started praying. The fact is that Daniel continued to pray even after God had answered the prayer. Whatever Daniel continued to pray afterwards was not determining whether God would answer the prayer or not for God had already answered before Daniel finished praying! All that Daniel prayed afterwards could not influence or affect God. What he said afterwards likely affected his receiving the answer. He affected the angel getting the answer to him.

Here are a few facts to consider again:

Daniel started his prayer with the discovery of the promise of God. The Word of God is the substance of Daniel's prayer. God's Word is a container of spiritual power (Heb. 1:3).

Daniel was not bitter or hard-hearted because of the trauma of captivity. Therefore, Daniel was not imposing any spiritual blockade that would hinder him from receiving the manifestation of the answer to his prayer. Had he been bitter or hard-hearted, his own hard heart would have blocked the release of the power contained within the prophetic Word. The Word would still be powerful but his hard heart would forbid its manifestation.

Daniel understood from Jeremiah's prophecy that in the mind of God, Israel was free from the shackles of their oppressors. They were still in bondage because there was no man to change that freedom from its spiritual form into natural form. When Daniel received understanding, he commanded the manifestation of the promise into being.

The testimony of the angel shows that the answer was released as quickly as Daniel spoke the Word in prayer and well before Daniel had even finished the prayer.

God would have said, "I have already answered Daniel's prayer".

If we were to ask the angel, Gabriel would have said, "God has answered. I am the one transporting God's answer to Daniel".

Those in Daniel's inner circles, who were watching him pray would have said, "Daniel is waiting on God to answer the prayer, it is taking time".

The spiritual man would explain to Daniel's friends, "Daniel was not waiting on God to answer. It was God that was waiting on Daniel to accept delivery of the answer in the visible dimension where man has authority".

The matter was out of God's hands, for He had answered instantly. The ministry of angels was involved in transporting the answer to Daniel. There was a delay between God's giving the answer spiritually and Daniel's seeing some evidence in the natural. This delay was not down to God. It is down to the fact that our prayers commission other spiritual beings. Thus your prayer starts with you and God but gradually starts involving others. As this circle widens the probability of delay increases.

Manifestation of answers to prayer involve other parties

Daniel did not pray to Gabriel, he prayed to God. Gabriel did not answer Daniel's prayer. Gabriel was involved in manifesting the answer that God already gave. We choose the request we will make in prayer but we cannot choose the parties that will directly affect our experience of the manifestation of the answer. Manifestation of answers to prayer often involve angelic ministry who act as spiritual logistics or transport mechanisms for the delivery of the answer to us or its manifestation in the natural.

Daniel was still speaking in prayer when the angel arrived in his presence. Thus answers to prayer already exist as spiritual realities way before we have finished praying! God gave the command immediately Daniel started praying. You should know you have answers to your prayers before you finish praying.

Daniel noted that the angel was caused to fly swiftly. The angel did not arrive in Daniel's presence in the twinkle of an eye. Did this angel experience a time delay purely down to the mechanics of the universe? Could the angel have flown any faster? Are some angels faster than others? What part do the angels and their own limits of motion play in the process of the manifestation of answers to prayer to show up in the material realm?

The things that Daniel continued to do after his initial prayer prepared him to experience the angelic delivery of the answer in the natural realm. It would appear that whether the answer manifested for Daniel or not was going to depend on Daniel's actions as well as the swiftness of the angel's motion. God had actually answered way before Daniel saw the answer. The implication is that it was perfectly possible that although God had answered that prayer, Daniel may have failed to receive the manifestation of that answer on the earth realm. There is a God-side to answered prayer and there is a man-side. Daniel received the manifestation after God had already said Yes. Even if Daniel had not received the manifestation it does not change the fact that God had answered in the spirit realm!

Logistics of answers to prayer

This story shows the parties that act together to produce the manifestation of answers to prayer. God gave the promise, which Jeremiah delivered as prophecy, and someone then wrote it down. Daniel saw the written Word and commanded manifestation of God's promise in the imperative mood, as a result of which God gave the answer in spiritual form. The angel then transported the answer to Daniel. Daniel continued with those actions that prepared him for receiving the answer in the natural realm.

Man determines manifestation

Let's say that as a fifteen year old, I am taught the spiritual secret of praying out the future plans of God. Let's assume that the cumulative of what I prayed out was the plans of God concerning my children and that I believed that God had answered me in the spirit realm. My need for growth, maturity and wisdom would constrain me from having a full manifestation of that prayer for a while. There is no delay on God's part. My growth is taking time. As part of my growth, I would complete my university education, start working, learn to make decisions, meet a girl I love and hopefully find that she loves me in return and agrees to marry me. We'll then learn to make a home together as man and wife before we set about having children. Even when my wife gets pregnant, she will have to carry the pregnancy to full term before the first baby is born!

It would be incorrect to hold the first baby in my arms and then exclaim, "At last, God has answered my prayer". God had answered that prayer many years before when I prayed as a teenager. That baby in my arms is a manifestation of the answer God already gave me in my teens. My relative inexperience did not stop God answering me immediately but it dictated how swiftly the manifestation could show up in my world. The cumulative of my choices over time released the manifestation of the prayer that had been answered many years before by God.

If I was the type of fellow looking to marry a dress-size 6, 8-foot tall Christian sister, the relative scarcity of such girls means that I wait much longer before the manifestation comes. Someone has to give birth to such a girl. If I additionally desire and insist that this 8-foot Christian girl must also have been miss universe at age ten, I might find that I have blocked myself from receiving the manifestation altogether. My choices have cancelled out my ability to receive the manifestation within my lifetime. The choices we make before and after prayer influence manifestation of answers to prayers, but God always answers speedily.

Now consider another record from Daniel's prayer life.

In those days I Daniel was mourning three full weeks. I ate no pleasant bread, neither came flesh nor wine in my mouth, neither did I anoint myself at all, till three whole weeks were fulfilled. And, behold, an hand touched me, which set me upon my knees and upon the palms of my hands. And he said unto me, O Daniel, a man greatly beloved, understand the Words that I speak unto thee, and stand upright: for unto thee am I now sent. And when he had spoken this word unto me, I stood trembling. Then said he unto me, Fear not, Daniel: for from the first day that thou didst set thine heart to understand, and to chasten thyself before thy God, thy words were heard, and I am come for thy words. But the

*prince of the kingdom of Persia withstood me one and twenty days: but,
lo, Michael, one of the chief princes, came to help me; and I remained
there with the kings of Persia. Now I am come to make thee understand
what shall befall thy people in the latter days: for yet the vision is for many
days.*
Daniel 10:2-3, 10-14

As you read this, remember that Daniel did not have the
wonderful name of Jesus, nor was he seated in heavenly places
with Christ as the new creation man is. Daniel was not a Christian
because the Lord had not risen from the dead. He could not
expect to be strengthened with the might of God in his inner
man. The power that was available to Daniel was external to
him. For the saint, the power of God lives within and we have
dominion over demons.

In this episode, a three-week fast was involved. This fast could
not have been designed to influence God since the angel revealed
to Daniel that God had heard Daniel's prayer since the first day.
Gabriel was then sent in response to Daniel's words. The angel
said, "your words were heard", he did not say, "your fasting
was observed and I have come in response to your fast". The
angel had come in response to Daniel's words. It did not take
God three weeks to answer this prayer. God answered from the
beginning of Daniel's prayer. The angel did not say, "O Daniel
your case is chronic therefore God needs to retire to bed in
order to ponder on your case". Irrespective of what happened
over the next twenty days, the undeniable truth was that God
had answered from the first day!

Why does it appear that God answered Daniel in five minutes
in one instance and in another instance three weeks? The
assumptions hidden in that question are unhealthy. In both
cases, God heard and answered the prayers instantly. There
was zero variation in the time that it took God to answer. The

observable variation has to do with manifestation of answer to prayers. God is not the only factor involved in the process that ends with manifestation of the answer on the earth.

Demonic hindrance varies in effectiveness

*But the prince of the kingdom of Persia withstood me one and twenty
days: but, lo, Michael, one of the chief princes, came to help me; and I
remained there with the kings of Persia.*
Daniel 10:1

The angel Gabriel's commentary shows that there are other beings involved in hastening or hindering the manifestation of the answer to that prayer on the earth. In this instance, there was demonic hindrance imposed by the demonic prince of Persia that slowed down the angelic transport from reaching Daniel. Delays could indicate demonic hindrance.

These evil spirit beings existed when Daniel received his answer in minutes in the Daniel 9 example. They were not as effective then as they were in this scenario, when they mounted a twenty-one day resistance to stop Daniel from receiving the manifestation of the answer that God had already sent through the angel. The answer to the Daniel 9 prayer manifested in the visible dimension that quickly because satan was somewhat in the dark about that prayer. He is limited in knowledge therefore limited in efficiency. There are times that satan knows what is going on and other times that he does not. These demons cannot hinder God from answering. When they know what is going on, they mount their attack after God has released the answer towards us, specifically in the interval between God's answer and man's experience of that answer in the visible dimension.

More benefits than Daniel

In that day, Daniel could only appeal to God. He could not do anything directly about satan. Daniel did not have the indwelling of God or the supply of spiritual power within. God helped Daniel from the third heaven where God functions. This supply could be intercepted before it got through to Daniel. Unlike Daniel, God's answers are not external to us.

In the New Covenant, we are the temple of God therefore we do not pull power from the third heaven. God supplies power within our inner man and we release this power through the outer man into the material world. Our spirit corresponds to "heaven" and our soul corresponds to the earth realm. Our battle today is making sure "heaven's" supply gets to the "earth". All the strongholds and imaginations that slow down that transfer operate between the recreated spirit of man and his soul realm. Daniel did not have the indwelling of God or the supply of spiritual power within his spirit nor did he have the use of the name of Jesus. Therefore Daniel's prayer and fasting directed at God were the only things he could resort to. Daniel could not command the devil to stop in mounting the resistance that was hindering Daniel's manifestation. Daniel had a limited revelation about the Devil for starters and if he knew about the Devil, there was little he could do directly to limit him. He was limited to what the angels could directly accomplish. There was no redemption yet and the fear of death kept man in subjection to satan (Heb. 2:14).

Daniel's prayers energised the angelic transport to show up in Daniel's world. A lot happens after we pray and God has said yes. Remember that demons are unlike our Father God; they are unpredictable, inconsistent and are not as faithful as we like to think that they are. They are not always able to hinder because they are limited in knowledge and their scope. They do not know when they can succeed; therefore they don't always have their acts together. When they have their acts together, they cannot delay the manifestation forever. In one instance, Daniel received manifestation into the earth within five minutes and then in another prayer scenario, there was hindrance imposed by demons interfering. Through all this, Daniel continued to pray but he could not directly deal with this prince of Persia that was causing his delay. Today, we can.

12

THREE TENSES OF PRAYER

Every prayer has a past, present as well as a future component to it. The future aspect is the one most people are interested in, for that is when you handle the manifested answer in the physical world.

Jesus had just cursed the fig tree. He then used this to explain the way the faith of God operates in relation to our asking, believing and receiving.

> *And Jesus, answering, saith to them, "Have the faith of God 24*
> *Therefore I tell you, whatever you ask for in prayer, believe that you have*
> *received it, and it will be yours.*
> *Mark 11.22,24 (WORRELL)*

A. S. Worrell's translation renders it, "Have the faith of God". God has given us His faith in the new creation.

Jesus had used the faith of God to destroy the fig tree by cursing it. On the back of that, Jesus taught us to release the faith of God by commanding the removal of the mountain. The faith of God releases the power that blasts the mountain out of our way. After moving the mountain, Jesus tells us to replace that mountain with our desires. Faith first commands the mountain to move and then faith speaks out your desires. For example, you'd command unforgiveness and strife to be uprooted from your home. That removes the mountain. You'd then release the ability of God's love to manifest as harmony in your home.

Greek scholars have pointed out that the aorist tense used in verse twenty-four actually means that our act of receiving precedes our act of asking. We are to believe that we have received before we even do the asking! We are asking in the present. We believe that we have received in the past. We will hold the manifested result in our hands in the future. When you hold the results in your hands you do not need to believe anyway for at that point you have something greater than believing. You know!

You are asking in the now.

You will have (the manifestation) in the future.

You have received in the past.

Take note of those tenses again for they are important. The asking is to follow after the believing. The believing aspect is what spans all the tenses. You believe before you ask, while you are asking and after you have asked up until you have manifestation. You believe that you have already received the answer in the kingdom of God within you.

Jesus teaches that answers to prayer in the material world are not really about God directly changing things in the physical.

He leaves the "having" to us. We are the ones that change and influence things in the physical plane. Jesus does not teach, "Pray and watch God change things". He teaches the relationship between what you believe and how that shapes what will manifest in your world in the future as a result of answers to your prayers. Receiving is not in the future but in the past (in the finished work of Christ), while having is in the future. We will later have (in the physical) what we have already received (in the spiritual).

Jesus does not only teach the importance of believing. He teaches us what should be the content of our believing in the place of prayer. We are not to believe that God will answer our prayer. We believe that we have already received the answer of God! We believe that God has already answered in the past.

Answers come in two stages

The principle is that we are praying because we have received by faith. The praying is to lead up to the manifestation of what we already received. Praying is the bridge between receiving in the past and having in the future.

Answers to prayer come about in two stages. The first stage is a reception into the kingdom of God within you. This reception is not perceptible to your physical senses. It is a reception by your spiritual senses. It is an actual reception in the dimension of "things not seen" in the invisible realm. The second stage of reception follows after the first stage and is a reception out of that inward kingdom into the material world where your hands can lay hold of the answer. You are receiving in the realm of "things seen". When many people talk about answers to prayer, they really are referring to the second stage of reception, the manifestation stage. Receiving in the kingdom of God within you is the primal and pivotal stage of reception. This first reception in the unseen realm gives foundation for receiving answers to prayer in the material world where the need exists.

If when I pray, I keep watching out for the expression of the answer in the physical world, I might not necessarily experience that which I am waiting for. This is because I have hindered myself by failing to do first things first. I must first believe that I have already received the answer to my prayers in a spiritual form into the kingdom of God within me. Failing to believe this, I start receiving doubts. These doubts prevent me from experiencing the second stage. It is very much like trying to build a roof on a house without walls. When I believe that I have already received the answer in invisible form into my heart, I release the power of God that works to turn invisible things into material equivalents in the material world.

God's side and man's side

For the grace of God that bringeth salvation hath appeared to all men,
Titus 2.11

In all of God's dealings with man, there is a divine side as well as a human side - Grace is God's side. Notice the tense, "hath appeared", that's the past tense. This means that God's side is already done. God is now resting. Failing to understand the importance and nature of the divine side causes people to spend the majority of their time trying to convince God into taking sides with them or giving something to them that He has not already given. God has brought salvation to all, so why are all not then saved?

There is a man side but man's side is a response to God's side.

Therefore it is of faith, that it might be by grace; to the end the promise might be sure to all the seed; not to that only which is of the law, but to that also which is of the faith of Abraham; who is the father of us all,
Romans 4:16

The purpose of faith is to fulfill God's grace. Faith is how we receive what God's grace has provided.

When you are trying to lead anyone to Christ, you do not use your feelings to validate the availability of saving power, do you? You do not find yourself asking whether the anointing is present or not in order that the lost one might be saved. You believe the report of God's Word. When we pray with the sinner today, we do not ask God to give us a sign. We have all the sign that we need in the death, burial and resurrection of the Lord Jesus from the dead. In the same way, your evidence that the prayer is answered is the fact that the Word says that in Christ Jesus we are already blessed with all spiritual blessings.

13

NEGLECTING THE ANSWER

G od has already said in His Word that by the stripes of Jesus we were healed (1 Pet. 2:24). Symptoms of sickness on our bodies do not prove that God is a liar. Jesus came to destroy the works of satan of which sickness is one (1 John 3:8). All that Jesus did, was God in Christ reconciling us to Himself (2 Cor. 5:19). Therefore God is unable to permit what He already personally disallowed in Jesus. Otherwise Jesus and God would be at odds with one another. Jesus is God's way of letting us know that He has outlawed evil. Jesus is God's pre-response with a thumping "Yes" to prayers that are based on His Word.

Though Jesus is God's "Yes", many Christians are still unsuccessful in prayer. Some trying to make sense of an unsuccessful prayer life have asked, "Why does God not permit us to see results for our prayers?" They attribute to God what God has not attributed to Himself. God is not the one permitting (or not permitting) anything.

Let's frame the same question differently.

Why do we permit ourselves not to see results for our prayers?

We have a glimpse in the book of Hebrews.

The Danger of neglect

How shall we escape, if we neglect so great salvation
Hebrews 2:3a

This is an explanation of one major reason why in spite of possessing "so great salvation", Christians still suffer tragedies. Though a way of escape is available, we forfeit it through our neglect. When we neglect the "so great salvation", we crowd out God's protection, shrink the footprint of God's grace and invite the enemy to steal, kill and destroy. When we don't walk in the spirit we could end up reaping the consequences of some other person's neglect. There is supernatural immunity from these secondary harvests, if we learn to listen to the indwelling Teacher who will reveal the way of escape to us by our recreated human spirit. Neglect happens when we become dull to the input of the Holy Spirit, God's Word and the inward witness.

When we pray the Word, the Word contains the power to bring about its own fulfillment. As we see the truth of what Christ has already accomplished through hearing the Word, faith rises up within to release power for manifestation. However through neglect, we permit the suspension of the manifestation of the answers to our prayers.

Consider this example from Hosea.

*When Israel was a child, then I loved him, and called my son out of
Egypt. I taught Ephraim also to go, taking them by their arms; but they
knew not that I healed them.*
Hosea 11:1, 3

God taught Ephraim spiritual truths about his true condition in
God. Though Ephraim was loved, taught and healed of God he
remained unaware of it. His neglect of God's teaching robbed
him of the enjoyment of healing. It is possible to be healed by
God and the one who is healed not know it! This is because
healing from God exists in the form of "things not seen". It
comes to us invisibly.

*Now we have received, not the spirit of the world, but the spirit which is
of God; that we might know the things that are freely given to us of God.*
Corinthians 2:12

In that verse, in both cases, the "s" in spirit is lowercase. This is
correct. This "spirit that is of God" refers to the human spirit
and not the Holy Spirit. Through our born again spirit we come
to know the answers that God has already merged into our lives.
If we believe that we do not have the answers, then our believing
makes God a liar. We would have believed the devil's lies that
answers to our prayers are in the distant future. The truth is
that God has already freely given us these answers in spiritual
form but wrong thinking dulls us to these realities within the
spirit man. It is because we do not understand God's true nature
that we pray incorrectly. Can we say "Abba Father" and "Oh
Problems" within the same sentence? Only the double-tongued
will cry out Abba Father one minute and "I am finished", the
very next. Those kinds of words neglect the great salvation
while shutting the way of escape. Our words have the power to
cancel out our praying.

A three-fold knowing

Let's look at an example of New Testament prayer:

Cease not to give thanks for you, making mention of you in my prayers; That the God of our Lord Jesus Christ, the Father of glory, may give unto you the spirit of wisdom and revelation in the knowledge of him: The eyes of your understanding being enlightened; that ye may know what is the hope of his calling, and what the riches of the glory of his inheritance in the saints, And what is the exceeding greatness of his power to us-ward who believe, according to the working of his mighty power
Ephesians 1:16-19

Paul prayed that their eyes of understanding open up, so that they would have a three-fold knowing of what is already theirs. Firstly, you are to know the hope of God's calling. Secondarily, you are to know the riches of the glory of His inheritance in the saints; and lastly you are to know the exceeding greatness of His power towards you in Christ.

We pray that Christians come to know the hope of God's calling. We do not ask God to give them another hope or calling. We pray because we know that God has already called them and that there is hope within that call. Our prayer is that these believers know what is already given in that hope.

Paul's prayer for a three-fold knowing for the Ephesians shows that it is possible to have and not know what it is that you have from God. This is the reason for the spirit of wisdom and revelation. Effective prayer starts when we know what God has already given us in Christ. Too often we frame our prayers as though God has not blessed us. The spirit of wisdom and revelation stops us from asking God to do those things that He says are already done. God has already supplied the answers in Christ. The answers are in your life. Unbelief admits that we have Christ but not the answers. Therefore unbelief uses prayer to psyche God into giving that which we do not already have.

The real focus in prayer is our becoming sure of the spiritual provisions of God. First, we know what we have been given in spiritual form, and then we receive the wisdom to change that provision into its material equivalent. Our starting assumptions in prayer must not make God out to be a liar.

For God doth know that in the day ye eat thereof, then your eyes shall be opened, and ye shall be as gods, knowing good and evil.
Genesis 3:5

God already said that Adam and Eve were created in God's image and likeness (Gen. 1:27). They were already like God. Satan lied to them that they were not. They received satan's lie, believed it and doubted God. When we harden ourselves against God's truth, we empower satan to lie to us. Believing a lie magnifies satan while shrinking the landscape for experiencing God's goodness. By submitting to satan's lies, we start receiving desires that we do not need.

The guile of satan

But I fear, lest by any means, as the serpent beguiled Eve through his subtilty, so your minds should be corrupted from the simplicity that is in Christ.
2 Corinthians 11:3

Satan aims to trick even the praying believer today in exactly the same manner that he tricked Eve. Eve got into doubt and unbelief when she started desiring to become what God already said that she was by design. Satan's biggest trick is to complicate the simple facts. God tells us what is already ours but experience says otherwise, so we side in with experience.

First thing to notice is that satan's status quo is not one of force, for he has no force to exert for starters. His method is guile. The guile is two-fold.

You have what God says that you do not have

Satan convinced Eve that she was deficient. She was trying to get rid of something she did not possess for starters. The core of the prayers flowing out of most people's prayer life is the idea that they have the very things that God says they do not have. The serpent convinces them that God has to get His facts straight for the believer is a possessor of weirdness. Believers that fall for this then go about trying to get off their lives these things that they believe they have.

You don't have, what God says that you have

The other major way that satan lies to Christians is to assure them that they do not have what God already says that they have. Most Christians believe that if God guided them they would prevail in life. They ignore what the Word has to say about what is already theirs. They busy themselves in prayer, persuading God to guide them.

Let's imagine the following conversation between God and such a believer, who prays:

"Father God, you are the God and Father of my Lord Jesus, the God of the new creation and provider of all things. I come to you today in the name of Jesus asking that you will lead and guide me ....."

Right in the middle of that prayer God interjects, "Son, what are you doing?"

The believer, shocked that God does not recognise that he is praying says, "Well, Father it is obvious that I am praying. You said in Your Word for us to pray, so I am praying that You will guide me."

God replies, "Son, that's My point. You stand there appearing to quote my Word to me but you are not saying what I said."

Believer replies, "You have to help me out here, I am praying and You are interrupting my prayers with Your questions. Can you let me finish my prayers, so You do Your part by answering them?"

God smiles and said, "This conversation that we are having right now is prayer. You can perceive Me talking to you from within your spirit and I can hear you respond back to Me; that my son is prayer. What was it that you wanted Me to be quiet about while you concluded your supposed prayer?"

Believer in a daze responds, "Surely I was praying, how could you refer to it as supposed prayer? Are You implying that in spite of all my diligence to set aside time, I was not really praying?"

God continues, "I already said in My Word that I will never forsake you, so it does not help when you make it your prayer point that I should not forsake you. If I said I won't, then I will not. I really will grab any opportunity to talk with you, but I'd rather you make it easier for both of us by cutting out things that make it look like I need encouragement to do what I said I will do."

Believer says, "You mean I don't have to ask you to lead me, go with me, go ahead of me and guide me or anything of that sort?"

God hugs the guy and says, "Ha! Ha! At last I am getting through to you. Yes, I don't want you speaking that way. You call it prayer but I don't. It is prayer when you trust me to do what I said I would do. When next you are concerned about these things, just smile and whisper your thanksgiving to me and let me know that you are so glad that I fulfil My Word. I guide you all the time. That thrills me. Thanksgiving also awakens your spiritual senses to discern what I am already doing in you."

God continues, "Don't forget that I am your Father, and your provider. Therefore I always supply the direction and clarity that you need even when it is not obvious to you. Perhaps you can pray that you will be open to my guidance when it shows up. Now son, since you insist that you have been praying let's humour you. As per your initial prayer point, do you not know that I already lead you? There are fine tunings needed here and there but rest assured they are not on my side but yours. I don't plan to stop guiding you by My Spirit for you are all I have, why will I not supply leadership to you?"

Believer says, "There are times I was convinced You were definitely with me because my feelings registered Your presence. When I don't feel Your presence it must mean that You are no longer there. This is why I am praying for You to be with me today."

God responds, "Feelings are a gift I have given you to enjoy but don't become a slave of your feelings. Sometimes the faith I deposited within you will produce feelings in you and at other times there will be no accompanying feeling. At such times, I want you to choose to operate by spiritual logic and shift from feelings to perceiving me by faith."

Believer says, "I think I get it now. You mean I should let You dwell in my heart by faith and not by feelings."

God whispers, "Yes son, yes, yes and yes! I am always there; already there, ever there with you. If you have to go by assumptions at all, go with the assumption that I am there. It is as you understand My love for you that the door to understand

Me will open up for you."

Believer whispers, "Thank you my Father God."
God winks at the Believer and laughs.

God is Your Father. Don't ask Him to be a father to you. He is the God and Father of the new creation man in Christ. As Father, He will guide you, so you don't need to ask Him to. Your prayer should focus on your end of the equation. God always fulfils His part but you need to know what He has done.

14

PRAYING THE
IMPLANTED WORD

The sower soweth the Word. And these are they by the way side, where the
Word is sown; but when they have heard, Satan cometh immediately, and
taketh away the Word that was sown in their hearts. And he said, So is
the kingdom of God, as if a man should cast seed into the ground; And
should sleep, and rise night and day, and the seed should spring and grow
up, he knoweth not how.
Mark 4:14-15,26-27

We can learn things about the proper execution of prayer as we consider the parable of the sower and the seed.

Jesus said that the knowledge of the secrets of the kingdom of God have been imparted through the understanding of this parable. The parable teaches that God's Word is THE universal spiritual seed that meets any need. Our human heart is the ground that forms the environment for the seed of God's Word to germinate. You put the kingdom of God into operation by planting the seed of God's Word into your own heart. Harvest flows from the seed of God's Word getting planted into the heart. Moreover the manifestation of the answer does not happen all at once but in stages and degrees (See Mk. 4:28).

You plant God's Word into your heart by saying it out of your own mouth. In that sense prayer is how you water the ground and the seed that is planted within it. You plant by confession and you water by prayer.

When men plant seed in farmlands, the seed is below the surface, invisible to the naked eye but that's where the seed works best. Most of the work that a physical seed does is underground before it starts shooting out of the ground. The seed keeps changing its form while under the soil until a critical mass is produced that breaks through the soil above the ground. At that stage, all eyes can see it. In order for eyes to see it, it had to have been allowed to operate invisibly for a while. The kingdom of God is invisible but produces physical effects in the natural realm.

Just as it is with a seed, God's kingdom starts from the invisible realm, from where it penetrates into the natural sphere. You speak God's Word out of your mouth in order to plant faith in your heart. You then water the seed of God's Word planted into the soil of your heart through speaking more words as confession and prayer. This parable teaches us not to conclude that just because we did not see changes overnight in the natural, then the watering of the seed of God's Word with prayer is not working.

This deceptively simple parable shows that abundance of soil does not imply a mighty harvest. More importantly, good soil with a lot of water does not yield a harvest. This means that while prayer is good, praying works best when the seed of God's Word is in the ground of your heart. Prayer waters the seed of God's Word that is already sown in your heart. The seed contains the image of what shall be. God's Word is the image of what shall be and it is the container of power. Prayer is not the "power" though it is a tremendous help for the release of power. Prayer releases the power that is within the Word. Without seed in the ground, a lot of watering yields a harvest of mud! No smart farmer wants to reap the mud on his farmland. Farmers want to harvest the plants produced by seeds and not water. You don't plant the prayer in that sense; you plant the seed of God's Word. You do not reap the praying you reap the seed sown.

Praying to God is watering the seed of God's Word, so that the power within the Word is released in your heart. The ground (the heart) is the production centre. It causes a harvest of whatever remains planted within it. What is manifested as answers has to be whatever has been sown within the heart in the first instance. When we pray, it is not some power locked up in the heavenly plane that we are waiting to release. We are releasing the power within the indestructible seed of God's Word planted in our hearts. Praying without storing the Word in your heart is an abuse of prayer. You converse best with God by making His Word the content of prayer.

Happy are you when you understand that time spent planting the Word into the heart is also part of prayer. Learn to prioritise the planting of God's Word in your heart daily as part of the daily practice of prayer. When prayer hits our heart and meets the Word of God there, it works tirelessly to release the power of God within His Word. When you are praying, you are really commanding the power within the Word to break out.

If prayer is not a product of the implanted Word, you will mostly pray amiss. When God tells us to first get the seed in the ground before watering it with prayer, He means that we should not start praying just because there is a situation at hand that needs correcting. If you do that you will unconsciously be watering the seed of the problem and causing it to grow through the attention you are giving the problem. You do not want to pray the problem; you want to pray the answer, which is the Word of God.

The Lord Jesus taught in the parable of the sower that whenever the hearing of the Word is not followed up with understanding, satan comes immediately to steal the Word that was heard (Mt 13:19). Satan is not afraid of you per se. He is afraid of the Word in you. It is because he is afraid of the Word in you that he immediately comes to steal the Word in your life. He steals through strongholds. These strongholds do not refer to spirit dominions over hills, valleys or cities. It refers to satan reigning wherever men reason against the Word in ignorance, unbelief and darkness (Acts 26:18). A Stronghold is the protection you give to unbelief.

Traditions and strongholds

The traditions of men that we hold onto render the Word ineffective (Mk 7:13). These traditions of men are actually doctrines of devils. Since the Bible itself provides instruction on the operations of demons, the doctrines of devils are not teachings about satan, demons or their operations. The doctrines of devils are the philosophies and sophisticated sounding logic that cause men to reason like satan and wallow in unbelief (2 Cor. 10:5). The Holy Spirit wants to reveal Christ in you and to you. Don't ask Him "Please show me what I am doing wrong". It is the law that gives the knowledge of sin (Rom. 3:20). That prayer is asking to be back under the law. Worse still it multiplies condemnation and guilt (Rom. 3:19), which is the ministry of death. Asking the Holy Spirit to show you all the wrong you are doing is asking to be ministered to by death (and Christians wonder why they never see the blessings manifest?). The very things people say out of ignorance of God's Word in the place of prayer could be ministering death to them slowly over time.

Many Christians pray but on their own terms and often powered by deep seated strongholds watered and nurtured through millennia of religious thought that are contrary to the knowledge of Christ. These ideas swim unchallenged in our head and contribute to the strongholds that weaken our belief in a good God. Strongholds are ideas and philosophies and any sophistry that exalts itself against the knowledge of Christ in us (See 2 Cor. 10:5). We are to cast down strongholds. This casting down of strongholds is the overthrow of limiting beliefs through the seed of God's Word planted within our heart. Those stories of Old Testament kings tearing down idols are a type or parable of the believer's effectiveness in pulling down strongholds. In the New Testament an idol is anything that diminishes your dependency on the faith of Christ. Real faith rests on the work of Christ based on what He has accomplished. This empowers your consciousness of the invincibility of Christ within you to meet all and any situation. Whatever belief does not stir that consciousness is a limiting belief and a stronghold that needs to be aggressively cast down by you. A belief that limits your comprehension of who God is, will without fail hinder you from knowing who you are because you are one spirit with Him (1 Cor. 6:17).

The real tragedy of strongholds is that whatever we believe about God does not change Him, angels or the devil even. It changes us. Whatever blocks you from having a clear view of our Father God and what He has accomplished in His Son will also leave you in a fog about what you truly are and how you should really pray. Until a stronghold is cast down, we continue to be hindered by what we already believe as a result of that stronghold. Strongholds hinder us from reaping God's answers to prayer.

God is good, able, willing, ready with His ability at our disposal but the fact is that there are many stories that make you go, "but if you say God is good, and ready what of so and so". These become the feeder system to the strongholds that build in our thoughts and imagination until they limit and restrict us from seeing and acting properly. These strongholds are destroyed only when we see Christ and continue to gaze on Him. The answer to whatever aims to perplex or confuse us is on the face of Jesus (See 2 Cor. 3:18).

15

PRAYING IN LINE WITH THE CHURCH AGE

And in that day ye shall ask me nothing. Verily, verily, I say unto you,
Whatsoever ye shall ask the Father in my name, he will give it you.
Hitherto have ye asked nothing in my name: ask, and ye shall receive, that
your joy may be full.
John 16:23-24

When the Lord Jesus said, "in that day", He was prophesying about the day ushered in by His resurrection. No one could pray in His name until after His resurrection. He was signalling a radical change in prayer to his disciples. The death, burial and resurrection of Jesus changed the rules governing our praying. Our approach in prayer in the New Covenant is different from the method of approach in the Old Testament. Jesus does not promise to relay our prayer to God (John 16:26). Jesus is the first-born son. Praying in His name means praying as sons just as He is a son because through the new nature we have also been given a new position as sons with the Father because we were raised together with the Son of God. We come to our Father directly in prayer because God treats us as His sons. Praying in His name is praying conscious that when we pray, the Father knows that because of sonship we are equal to Jesus.

Asking in His name does not just mean ending our prayers with the mantra "In Jesus name, amen". That phrase is a portable way of summarizing our rights to receive from the Father because we have been made joint heirs with the first-born. It means that we are now sons in exactly the same way that He is a son of the Father through receiving the new nature. To pray, "In my name", means to pray convinced that the provision has already been made through the cross of Christ. God has supplied all that we'll ever need in the form of resurrection power, which now resides within every son of God. Now it is up to us to use it by releasing that power through our authority.

There is a story told of Friedrich Myconius, Martin Luther's assistant in the sixteenth century. Myconius became sick to the point that death was clasping its cold hands on him. Friedrich was certain that this was death's call and that his time of ministry was up on the earth, so he sent a farewell note to Luther. Luther received the letter and instantly sent back the following reply:

"I command thee in the name of God to live. I still have need of thee in the work of reforming the church. The Lord will never let me hear that thou art dead but will permit thee to survive me. For this I am praying, this is my will, and may my will be done because I seek only to glorify the name of God."

Martin Luther spoke those words in 1540! The first time I read them, the audacity of those words killed the Goliath of unbelief in me. One week after Myconius heard Luther's reply he recovered. Interestingly, as per the command of Luther, Myconius died two months after the death of Luther.

What Jesus said from Heaven

After His ascension to heaven, the Lord Jesus taught us more about prayer through the prayers of Paul. Paul addresses God in prayer in a whole new light. Though he was a Jew, in his prayers for the believers at Ephesus, Paul approached God not as the God of Abram, Isaac and Jacob but as the God of our Lord Jesus Christ. These terms are not Jewish. He prayed as a Christian and not as a biological Jew.

The thrust of those New Testament prayers is that Whatever is subject to the Head is subject to us too as members of that same body. In those prayers we find that the same resurrection power that raised Jesus from the dead is with our spirits. That power is ours to use now. It is through our recreated spirits that we receive the riches of what the Father has already accomplished in translating us from death to life.

Pray in response to God's movements

Grace be to you, and peace, from God our Father, and from the Lord Jesus Christ. Blessed be the God and Father of our Lord Jesus Christ, who hath blessed us with all spiritual blessings in heavenly places in Christ: According as he hath chosen us in him before the foundation of the world, that we should be holy and without blame before him in love: Having made known unto us the mystery of his will, according to his good pleasure which he hath purposed in himself:
Ephesian1:2-4, 9

God's mercy has already caused Him to make His moves in

Christ. He did not move in response to our prayer. Instead, He asks us to pray in response to His movements! All that God did, He did because of the great love wherewith He loved us. There is much ground that God has covered that remains unenjoyed because what we believe hinders us from discovering His goodness. We must know and believe the revelation of God's goodness in order to enjoy it. Though goodness is there ready and available, it is not automatic. As we hear of what He has done, faith comes (Rom. 10:17). Faith then receives God's goodness in the unseen realm and transforms it into benefits that we enjoy in the visible dimension.

What if we doubt God's goodness? It does not diminish Him or cause Him to abandon goodness. He cannot be anything other than good. Unbelief prevents us from entering into the enjoyment of His goodness (Heb. 3:19). Unbelief moves us to depart from that goodness and also outlaws it in our experience while opening the avenue for man to co-create evil and permit its existence in the earth.

In the light of this, God inspired Paul to desire that the Spirit of wisdom and revelation in the knowledge of Him floods our eyes with light. This is so we can see God as He already is.

Paul does not ask God to love us, deliver us or give us redemption. The prayer takes it for granted that God has already lavishly provided all that and much more. The prayer focuses on something happening to us as the recipients and intended beneficiaries of God's great love. On the whole we are blind to the spiritual reality of this great love. You can often tell what a person really believes by the subject and content of their prayers, when they have their backs against the wall.

When our eyes are flooded with the light of God, we see Him.

When we see Him, we see all else for what they really are. God's intent is not that we see Him in the heavens, though the heavens belong to Him or in the universe at large, even though He is Lord of all. God intends that we see His nature within, see ourselves as He is and so we grow up into Him (2 Cor. 3:18). The prayers of Paul don't sound like the prayers that 99.99% of the church prays today in private as well as public gatherings. His prayers call us to pray as those sitted with Christ on a higher plane where we already possess all things.

Cease not to give thanks for you, making mention of you in my prayers;
That the God of our Lord Jesus Christ, the Father of glory, may give
unto you the spirit of wisdom and revelation in the knowledge of him:
Ephesians 1:16-17

Paul prayed for these Ephesians because he had already unfolded the Word to them.

One of the startling things about the prayers of the Bible in general and the prayers of the epistles in particular, is that they prayed about the cause and not the effects. For example, they did not pray about money or the likes. They knew money was an effect. Money follows the blessing of God. Riches and honor are an effect of wisdom (Prov. 8:18). Solomon directly received wisdom from God and as a result attracted enough wealth to become the richest man in the world. Money mistakes are the product of the neglect of wisdom. Therefore cooperating with the wisdom of God will manifest wealth and correct money problems. This wisdom is of the spirit. This is what Paul majors on in his prayers. Again, the saints prayed from the spiritual standpoint. The infinite supply already available in the spirit was their reality. They would major on walking in the joy of the Lord in their prayers because a merry heart is pure medicine. You'd not find sick people who are overflowing in joy. Healing is the effect but the joy of God is the cause (Prov. 17:22).

Our eyes must be flooded with light enough to yield to the wisdom and grace of God within us. Usually, when we stop seeing wisdom and grace, it pressures us into poor money decisions. We then try to use prayer to plug the money draining away from our lives, instead of seeing more of and increasing our response to the wisdom of God. Wisdom is a spiritual substance that we respond to and as a by-product release material abundance in the natural plane.

I was startled the first time I saw the fact that the Christians that Paul is praying for are people that already had heard the gospel captured in the first fourteen verses of Ephesians. When he prays for "the spirit of wisdom and revelation in the knowledge of him", he is not referring to more knowledge which comes as a form of teaching given from the pulpit. He is praying about acknowledgement on the part of the believer. Once taught the truths of redemption, the believer needs the help that is supplied through prayer in order to let that knowledge shape what he acknowledges.

Praying with Paul

There are different dispensations in the Bible and when you see the prayers of an age in the Bible, you know what that age is about. A new dispensation really calls for a new emphasis in prayer. You must learn to pray in a manner consistent with the dispensation that the church lives under.

The pattern that we find is as follows:

1. First, God communicates the mystery of His will for the Church age to the believer through the epistles. This gospel, which reveals the mind of God for the Church age then becomes the knowledge that the believer

adjusts to. Each believer finds his place in that plan.

2. Once the believer had been immersed in this good news, Paul (the minister) prayed for that saint in line with God's plan for this age. That the believer's spiritual eyes open up to see the truths of the Church age in particular. Everything is already provided for according to the riches of God's grace.

3. In answer to this request, the power within the mystery produces spiritual vision. This causes the believer to see or acknowledge the specifics of the New Covenant that he had been taught.

4. The believer, whose eyes have been enlightened, is then encouraged to pray for Paul (the minister) so he has utterance to communicate more of the mysteries of God.

5. Thus the believer, who has been taught the mysteries of this age, influences the ministry of the minister who brought him into contact with the truths of God's Word, so the minister can make more of that truth known.

The prayer is to change the mind of the believer and not to change God's mind. Not once do you find Paul praying like Moses prayed telling God to repent (Ex. 32:14). It is the believer that repents by acknowledging the truth (2 Tim. 2:25). Repentance speaks of adjusting the soul to think the thoughts of God in the age of the mystery.

Moving from hearing to seeing

The eyes of your understanding being enlightened; that ye may know what is the hope of his calling, and what the riches of the glory of his inheritance in the saints,
Ephesians 1:18

In other words, the Spirit is saying through Paul, "I need to pray for you because you now know". He is not praying for the ones who have not heard. Christians don't need prayers until they have been exposed to New Testament truth. Once exposed to truth, prayer is needed so that our eyes are opened and our total outlook changes to line up with truth. Our eyes open in degrees. The measure to which you know the mystery of God's will changes your total outlook. This prayer effectively says "I have told you the mystery for this age. I won't tell you more just yet, for it is not more that you need to hear. Now you need to see more as a result of what you have already heard". The thrust of new creation praying is specifically that those that have been taught might start seeing and judging all things in the light of the specific truth for this age. This is because satan's deception is not broken by just hearing New Testament truth but by the believer acknowledging or recognizing it. To acknowledge the truth that we know means that we become deliberately influenced by what we see as a result of what we have heard. Until this happens, we neglect what it means to live in the church age and unconsciously live like we were back under dispensations gone before.

The end result of Paul's prayer in the first chapter of Ephesians is that we function as the fullness of Christ. The result of his prayer in the third chapter of Ephesians is that the believer is filled with the fullness of God.

These prayers are the templates of prayers for the church age. In the New Testament, if I say that I do not see a truth, it does not disprove the truth. It mostly reflects that I am blind. While it is true that I have eyes, I find myself denying what God has accomplished already. It is not acceptable not to see truth. Truth is not theory.

Living like you ought to

*Praying always with all prayer and supplication in the Spirit, and
watching thereunto with all perseverance and supplication for all saints;
And for me, that utterance may be given unto me, that I may open my
mouth boldly, to make known the mystery of the gospel, For which I am
an ambassador in bonds: that therein I may speak boldly, as I ought to
speak.*
Ephesians 6:18-20

The book of Ephesians is to the Christian what the book of
Exodus was to those under the Law. It is a documentation of
the life of the new creation man. In it, we find a framework for
praying like those who live in the age of the mystery.

After Paul had given six chapters of pure revelation knowledge
in the book of Ephesians, which is his greatest epistle, he asks
for prayer. An Apostle needs the prayers of those who need
his ministry. Paul asks that prayer be made for him that he may
boldly make known the mystery of the gospel. This boldness
was beyond the natural disposition of Paul but an answer to
prayer! This man who had been in shipwrecks often, fought wild
beasts as well as successfully faced mobs, now requests prayers
so he'll be bold in speaking, as he ought to speak.

He does not request that he speak like Peter, James or John. He
had listened to enough of the mystery to know that there is a
way that he ought not to speak. It takes boldness to take your
place in the New Covenant, live and speak like you ought to.

Initially, Paul prays that each of his hearers may know the
mystery. Afterwards, he instructs those same believers to pray for
him that he may make known the mystery. The prayers that you
pray for your pastor, who feeds you the Word of God, actually
empowers you to know more of what God says is already done.

You are part of the answer to your prayers.

Growing by seeing more of him

No man hath seen God at any time, the only begotten Son, which is in the bosom of the Father, he hath declared him.
John 1:18

Jesus declares God perfectly because He has seen God. It is on the face of Jesus that we see God clearly for who He really is. Until Jesus, no man had seen the Father God. The Old Testament saints did not know the Father, though they did their best with what little veiled understanding of Him that they had. Therefore, their prayers contained themes that Jesus would not pray. There are many unscriptural prayers in the scriptures. We cannot just copy an Old Testament prayer simply because we find it in the Bible. Those were prayers uttered from seeing God dimly by men ruled by spiritual death.

God does not inspire Paul to pray for the saints that the universe be rearranged or that our external environment change. He does not even pray that the issues, travails and problems disappear. Answers already exist in Christ within the believer in the invisible realm. It is as we see Him clearly that we boldly command what we see in Him into manifestation. We grow by continuing to see more of Him and our true stature in His. Paul's prayer implies that a whole lot depends on the strength of our seeing and the object that we see. The secret is in seeing that the answer is living within us.

There are many believers seemingly groaning to generate faith for the situation at hand. The faith that is required is the faith that believes that the answer is in the eyes that are flooded with light to see the Lord. You don't need more faith than that required for seeing what God wants you to do. All else that we require flows from what we see when we see the Lord. Faith is a struggle until we yield to seeing correctly by seeing Him. Prayer therefore is opening up our inner eyes to see Him alone and to see all things as He sees them. We pray in order to see that God is enough by His supply through His life within us.

God does not need to do more, we just need to do less doubting, less unbelief and less mistrusting of God's availability, ability and willingness. The more we see, the less we doubt. Faith that flows from seeing the Lord basically handcuffs the unconscious doubt that causes us in prayer to keep asking God to do more. The faith that prays in the New Testament knows that the Cross of Christ transmits power for all eternity. Our vision causes the power to take the shape of our need. We then command the manifestation of what we see into being in the natural.

New Testament faith does not say, "I know I already have Christ, now I need peace, so I am asking God to give me peace". The peace of God is ever present with your spirit. When cares surface, we cast our cares on the Lord. Anxiety and frets block our vision of the peace within. You cast the cares and anxieties so as to remove the blocker stopping you from seeing the peace of God within. Once your vision is restored, you find the peace flowing out of your spirit into your heart (Philippians 4:7).

He that spared not his own Son, but delivered him up for us all, how shall
he not with him also freely give us all things?
Romans 8:32

New Testament faith does not say, "I know I already have Christ, now I need healing, so I am asking God to heal me". It says, "Since I have Christ, I already have healing for Christ is healing and health to me (1 John 5:12)". We pray in order that our eyes open to the truth that all that we need exists in Christ and is already supplied as power to us. As we release this exceeding great power through our actions and our command, it becomes healing in our body.

New Testament faith is access to all the spiritual blessings that God has blessed us with. The blessing exists as power in the invisible realm. It is pivotal that through revelation knowledge, we acknowledge that this power is within our spirits just as it was housed in Jesus. We treat our spirits like Power Stations. Our prayer permits us to continue to see things this way. We are not asking God to move again. Our prayers deliberately cause POWER to flow out of our bellies as we exercise faith. It is up to us to transmit this power as needed.

16

GOD ANSWERS IN THE INNER MAN

When I think of the greatness of this great plan I fall on my knees before God the Father (from whom all fatherhood, earthly or heavenly, derives its name),
Ephesians 3:14 (Message)

Our Father's family lives in two domains. The earthly and the heavenly. It's just like a rich man who has a winter house in the Caribbean but spends all his summer months in London. Family remains unchanged by location. In the light of the family fact, we know that as sons we do not petition our Father God before He provides for us. When you approach God in prayer, remember that you are family. More often than not, all that we remember is that we have a need. We must allow the Holy Spirit convict us of the Father-fact. There is no need for a covenant between the Father and His family before He meets our needs. As believers we obtain from our Father based on sonship. In healthy families, sons approach the table knowing there will be provision. Sons don't make deals with their Father in order to eat at His table.

Prayer releases power

The earnest prayer of a righteous man has great power and wonderful results.
James 5:16 (TLB)

The prayer of a person living right with God is something powerful to be reckoned with.
James 5:16b (Message)

Tremendous power is made available through a good man's earnest prayer.
James 5:16b (JB Phillips)

The earnest (heartfelt, continued) prayer of a righteous man makes tremendous power available [dynamic in its working].
James 5:16b (AMP)

The power that prayer makes available is not based on the prayer itself but on the gift of righteousness. Through the gift of righteousness God supplies strength to the ungodly (Rom. 5:6). Since you are God's righteous one you are to believe that your prayer makes tremendous power available. Prayer is a means of releasing that power into our own daily living. As we understand righteousness, the very act of praying releases the power of redemption.

James sheds more light on his teaching about prayer:

And if, in the process, any of you does not know how to meet any particular problem he has only to ask God who gives generously to all men without making them feel foolish or guilty—and he may be quite sure that the necessary wisdom will be given him. But he must ask in sincere faith without secret doubts as to whether he really wants God's help or not. The man who trusts God, but with inward reservations, is like a wave of the sea, carried forward by the wind one moment and driven back the next. That sort of man cannot hope to receive anything from God, and the life of a man of divided loyalty will reveal instability at every turn.

James 1.5-8 (JB Phillips)

If you don't know what you're doing, pray to the Father. He loves to help. You'll get his help, and won't be condescended to when you ask for it. Ask boldly, believingly, without a second thought. People who "worry their prayers" are like wind-whipped waves. Don't think you're going to get anything from the Master that way, adrift at sea, keeping all your options open.

James 1:5-8 (The Message)

God is a giver. He gives all things to us through His power. He gives wisdom to this man in the form of spiritual power.

In this scenario, a child of God has prayed but God does not answer his prayer (If you have been following the teaching in this book you know that is not true. We ask because we already know that the answer is pre-approved in God). If our prayer is scriptural, the challenge in prayer is that the Christian often fails to receive the answer. It is not about God not answering. How can God "un-answer" what He has already said 'Yes' to in Christ? (2 Cor. 1:20)

James lets us see that prayer is not about leaving your requests in the hand of God, assuming that it is up to Him whether it is answered or not. This man is asking about God's wisdom but he is not really asking properly, therefore he does not receive. You can pray for perfectly legitimate things and still fail to receive answers to your request. James does not teach that God withholds. He shows how a man can disqualify himself from receiving. When a man prays to God, the element of doubt in his own heart cancels the release of God's power, which would have brought forth manifestation of his request. This double minded man by the instability in his mind and his unwillingness to make up his mind about God's goodness is releasing doubt which handcuffs the power of God in his heart! God has provided Christ as wisdom. God cannot undo that. The man is praying but his doubt is stopping power from changing to wisdom. Prayer does not automatically work to release power. The presence of faith causes power to change to wisdom. Doubt in the heart shackles faith in the heart and stops wisdom from manifesting. When that happens the man is unable to receive.

James does not say that prayer makes the sick whole. He says it is the prayer offered in faith. It is faith that makes prayer work. Prayer is a means of releasing faith and faith then releases the power of God. The Lord Jesus provides both the faith and the power and leaves it up to us to put that power to work as we operate in faith.

When James says that the prayer of a righteous man releases tremendous power, in context he is really saying that it is the faith of God housed within the words of the praying man that releases tremendous power of God. Prayer is an avenue of releasing the faith of God through the spoken words of our mouth as they line up with God's holy Word.

The postcode of power

Grace and peace be multiplied unto you through the knowledge of God, and of Jesus our Lord, According as his divine power hath given unto us all things that pertain unto life and godliness, through the knowledge of him that hath called us to glory and virtue:
2 Peter 1:2-3

God's supply is in His grace. You can multiply God's grace to yourself as you gain knowledge of what the Lord Jesus has accomplished in redemption. You are multiplying the grace for the benefit of your soul. The more you know of what Jesus has done, the greater the peace of God deposited in your soul.

It is not only important to know that God gives to us, it is crucial to know how He gives. God gives to us through His divine ability. God's divine ability has already given you all that you will need in this life. Whatever you want, He gives to you in power form. Your faith then transforms this power-form of things into their material equivalent.

Peter continues along the same line and says:

> *Whereby are given unto us exceeding great and precious promises: that by these ye might be partakers of the divine nature, having escaped the corruption that is in the world through lust.*
> *2 Peter 2:4*

God supplies us by giving us power. God does not take this power back nor does He withdraw it. It remains with your spirit forever. God also gives to us through the precious promises of His Word, which are fulfilled in Christ Jesus. The promises of God's Word as well as God's power are mechanisms of supply from God. They are one and the same thing.

Power and faith transmitter

When you receive the gospel, you have received God's power (Rom 1:16). Power is hiding within every utterance of God. The Word of God therefore transmits power just as well as it transmits faith. Think of God's Word as both a faith transmitter and a power transmitter. You need to be as aware of the power as you are of the faith, for both work together to manifest change. We release this self-fulfilling power within God's promises through knowledge of the truth. The act of believing the gospel releases the effects of salvation into our lives. It also releases the power already contained within God's promise.

The level of renewing of our minds regulates how much of that power is released to meet our need. Therefore, it is not up to God if the power is unleashed or not. We are responsible for receiving the manifestation of God's promises. God does not determine the manifestation of answers to prayers; we do. If we do not doubt, faith releases the power of God, which He has given to us through His precious promises. If we doubt, we handcuff ourselves and prevent the manifestation (Mk. 11:23).

For when we were yet without strength, in due time Christ died for the ungodly
Romans 5:6

The unbeliever is a man without strength. God solved this problem of being "without strength" by having Christ die for ungodly men. The New Birth is therefore, the reception of strength within the inner man because we believed and confessed Christ's death and resurrection. The power in a Christian's life is the same power that raised Jesus from the dead. This power was hidden in the gospel and released into the human spirit of the one who heard and believed the gospel.

God is a Spirit.
John 4:24a

God is a pure Spirit. He does not have a physical body or any biological or psychological component. We therefore, cannot relate to Him biologically, chemically or from a physical standpoint. While God does not currently control the visible realm, He retains the control of the invisible realm, the unseen realm (Ps. 115:16).

Brethren, the grace of our Lord Jesus Christ be with your spirit. Amen.
Galatians 6:18

The last thing that Paul told the Galatian Church was that the grace of God was already present in their lives. This grace is not directly with our brain, emotions, feelings, or senses. Grace is of the spirit. It produces results in the physical, but it is not physical. God's grace is with our human spirit and operates in the unseen realm beyond the physical senses. Except you prioritize your spirit man, you would frustrate God's grace that it is present within you.

The Lord Jesus Christ be with thy spirit. Grace be with you. Amen
2 Timothy 4:22

When we are leaving our friends, we usually say the really important things last. The last thing that Paul wrote to Timothy was this, "The Lord Jesus is with thy spirit". We are united with Christ through our recreated spirit. The grace of God as well as the presence of Jesus functions through the spirit of man. Jesus functions through your human spirit.

And the very God of peace sanctify you wholly; and I pray God your
whole spirit and soul and body be preserved blameless unto the coming of
our Lord Jesus Christ.
1 Thessalonians 5:23

In describing the anatomy of the whole man, Paul mentions the three dimensions of our being as spirit, soul and body. The order implies that when God gets involved with our lives He does not start in the body. God starts His activity in the spirit of man and from there works outward from the invisible realm. This means that God indirectly intervenes in the seen realm through the human spirit. He begins where He has authority. He begins with the spirit of man. The deposits of God are within the human spirit. The spiritually conscious Christian then works that power from the spirit out into the physical dimension through the principles of faith.

Kingdom supply

And hath made us kings and priests unto God and his Father; to him be glory and dominion for ever and ever. Amen.
Revelation 1:6

The Lord Jesus has constituted us as kings and priests unto our God. Since we are kings, where is the kingdom?

Jesus prayed, "Thy kingdom come". (Mt. 6:10)

Jesus also taught His disciples, "Seek first the kingdom of God and his righteousness …" (Mt. 6:33)

Since Jesus said we should seek, He implies that we can locate the kingdom of God. It is our job to find the kingdom first.

The kingdom of God is His will being done on the earth so that earth becomes a copy of heaven. The kingdom of God is His righteousness given to men. Paul described the kingdom of God as, "Righteousness, peace and joy in the Holy Ghost" (Rom. 14:17)

During the 1,000 year earthly reign of Christ, the kingdom of God will physically manifest on earth in a visible way. Right now, we have that kingdom in its spiritual form within the spirits of every born again one. The kingdom of God is inside your born again spirit. Seeking the kingdom of God therefore does not refer to attending every religious convention in town. It means locating the ability of God within the reborn spirit.

And he lifted up his eyes on his disciples, and said, Blessed be ye poor: for
yours is the kingdom of God.
Luke 6:20

Jesus did not say people are blessed for being poor. Religion schools men into thinking that way but Jesus did not teach it. He said the poor that are blessed are the ones that have been given the kingdom of God. It is because they have been given the kingdom of God that they are blessed. The empowering to prosper is within the kingdom that has been given to man. We are to receive all our needs met out of this kingdom. The kingdom of God was given to the poor through the New Birth. We were made kings at the New Birth because we received a kingdom within our spirits.

The Lord Jesus gave further insight concerning this kingdom. He said that the kingdom of God is voice activated. You tap into the provisions of the kingdom of God within by planting the seed of God's Word into your heart (Mk. 4:26). God's Word is the treasure within your heart. Within your heart, it becomes the substance of all that you will ever need in life.

We have been translated out of the dominion of darkness (Col 1:13). In the place of prayer, we are to remember that kingdom ability is at work within us. Our role as kings is the release of that ability out of that inward kingdom. As we spend time in the Word, we gain knowledge of how to use that ability.

Every king has his own dominion. When you pray, you are receiving out of the dominion of God into your dominion as a king. We receive within us. Before you pray try picturing how the power that Jesus made available through His cross, He has deposited that same power within us as strength in the New Birth (Rom 5:6). Then anticipate that it will be released from within your spirit as you speak the Word of God in prayer (Ephesians 3:20). Train your soul to see this power flowing out into the environment around you to manifest change. Prayer is a means through which you are applying this available power of God that the Lord Jesus has supplied in redemption.

The heart

At the new birth, our spirits are born of the incorruptible seed of God's Word (1 Pet. 1:23). Since the human spirit is a product of God's incorruptible seed, it is incapable of sinning because the seed of God's Word remains within the spirit of man (1 John 3:9). There is no imperfection in the human spirit. The temptation to sin or to doubt can therefore never flow from the spirit of man. The Bible says some important things about the heart.

And immediately when Jesus perceived in his spirit that they so reasoned within themselves, he said unto them, Why reason ye these things in your hearts?
Mark 2:8

The repetition of heart and spirit is not simply there for emphasis. Mark goes to great lengths to use different Greek words to distinguish between the related concepts of spirit and heart in the same sentence. The spirit perceives while the heart reasons. Jesus is operating out of His spirit, while the disciples were operating out of their heart. This reasoning with the heart was within. This was not brain activity. The brain and the whole body are not part of the heart.

But let it be the hidden man of the heart, in that which is not corruptible, even the ornament of a meek and quiet spirit, which is in the sight of God of great price.
1 Peter 3:4

Heart and spirit are used together here in a clearer sense. The spirit of man is the hidden man of the heart. The spirit is not all there is to the heart. It is the incorruptible part of it. It is the part of the heart, which is of great price before God. We are to let our spirits govern our hearts. Our spirits are to be kings reigning within our souls.

Hosea speaks of a divided heart. He describes a heart embroiled in civil war. In a divided heart the spirit and the soul are unable to agree on a matter and are headed in opposite directions (Hosea 10:2).

In Mark 11:23, Greek scholars point out that the phrase "shall not doubt in his heart" is written in the passive voice. Thus the man who is commanding this mountain to move is receiving the doubt. This should therefore be translated as "shall not receive doubt in his heart". This heart that receives doubts cannot be a characteristic of the incorruptible reborn human spirit. Neither God nor the reborn spirit doubts. If we make heart there refer to spirit, we violate the principle that the seed of God within the human spirit means it cannot sin. Thus we must not always treat heart and spirit as equivalent terms. Clearly the heart can doubt, though the hidden man of the heart cannot; therefore the portion of the heart that can doubt has to refer to something other than the spirit. It is a reference to the soul. In its proper sense, believing is getting the soul to agree with our spirits about the Word of God. Doubting with the heart describes the soul that alternates between agreeing with the spirit and with the evidences of the physical world.

The heart is also described as impure (Jam. 4:8), evil (Mk. 7:21), dull, slow as well as good. The heart is not a fourth component to man. It is not another creation of God. It is a short way of describing the combination of soul and spirit. Trusting God with all our heart simply means that we are to align our soul with our spirit through the renewing of our mind! (Proverbs 3:5, Rom. 12:2). That phrase "all the heart" refers to spirit and soul together. Sometimes referred to as the inner man.

In order to manifest the already-complete salvation of the spirit in our daily walk, we need to engage the whole of our heart. Believing with all your heart refers to an operation where the belief within your spirit additionally affects your soul through the renewing of the mind (Rom 12:2). When that happens you believe with all your heart.

The concept of the heart helps us understand that the soul is the greatest limitation of the reborn spirit of man. If your mind is not renewed to God's Word, all the treasures within your spirit go untapped. When your soul agrees with your spirit, you are spiritual minded. The effect of the spiritual mind is life, peace and power (Rom. 8:6).

What is the function of the heart?

The heart aligns with the spirit or the world. The heart in its most potent form is not meant to receive things in from the world but to flow power out from the human spirit. We guard our heart diligently because out of it flows the issues of life (Prov. 4:23). Our heart is the medium through which treasures flow from our spirit into our soul. These issues start out in our spirit but are needed in the natural everyday world. In the new creation, the heart has access to the spirit. This access can become clearer and wider.

Your spirit man is already made complete in Christ (Col 2:10). In the new birth, we were given the vitality and ability of God, which is sealed, into our human spirit. The new birth is a birth into the strength of God. The Lord Jesus Christ relates to and puts the deposit of His grace within your spirit. Your human spirit is designed to govern the soul, body and the world around you. The human spirit does not directly govern the physical world except through the soul component of your heart. The grace within the spirit is needed in the soul component of your heart where transformation occurs.

Some Christians think that their problem is that they have head knowledge. They think that they want the knowledge deep down in their spirits. Truth is you want your mind renewed. At some point, your heart knowledge really needs to become head knowledge. This is because our struggle as believers is in our heads and not in our spirits. You need what's in your heart to get into your head. This is the next phase in getting our lives to turn around. What God has put into you needs to flow into your head and out of your mouth. Your role is to renew your mind, so that there is a free flow from spirit via soul through your spoken words into your circumstances.

God gives spiritually

When God gives to you, He gives spiritually for He is a spirit and His realities are spiritual in nature.

> *That he would grant you, according to the riches of his glory, to be strengthened with might by his Spirit in the inner man;*
> *Ephesians 3:16*

This inner man is sometimes called the inward man (2 Cor. 4:16). This inward man is still getting changed daily. Since our spirit is already created complete in Christ Jesus, it does not get renewed daily. Therefore, this "inward man" is not a reference to the reborn spirit. It is our soul that needs daily renewal. The inward man is like the gloves that the hidden man of the heart wears in order to express itself. The hidden man is the human spirit whereas the inward man more accurately describes the soul component of the heart submitted to the recreated spirit.

In order to experience what we know from the Word, strength must flow from the inner man. We are to pray for those that we know have been taught New Testament truth that they be strengthened with God's might. The resurrection power of God, already sealed by God into the human spirit at the new birth, should produce rebuilt character and transformed personalities in the Christian. It is possible that the power remains hidden and is so veiled that its effect on the total person is not seen. This is the abnormality that Paul is trying to counteract with these prayers. His desire is that through the human spirit governing the heart and the outer man, Christ manifests in our total man. The strengthening of God in the heart causes the heart to behave like the spirit; thus flooding man with the personality and vitality of God.

God's glorious riches are all spiritual in nature. He supplies these riches (answers) to us in the heavenly plane (Eph. 1:3). They show up in our lives as a form of strengthening in the inner man. This is fundamental.

God relates to us through our spiritual nature. As a spirit, His dealings are with other spirit beings. This means that when God answers your prayer, He gives the answer in spiritual form. God's supply comes as strength from His Spirit within our spirits into our inner man. God supplies the answer in the form of spiritual power in the unseen dimension via our spirit. Our need is in the physical dimension but the answer is in our unseen realm. We unconsciously think that God's answers are physical, chemical and biological just like our challenges are. God's answer is not material in nature. He relates to our spirits and not our brains, our feelings or even our problems.

The power working in us

God is a pure spirit being without a physical body. Man is like God in that he is a spirit being; in addition, man also has a physical component to him. You are the one that deals with physical materials and circumstances. God comes to the aid of our weaknesses and transfers spiritual substance to man by His grace because of His love. Man receives this spiritual substance within his inner man. Man then responds to God's grace through the principles of faith in God and His Word. Faith does not change God. It changes the spiritual substance of power into an equivalent physical form.

Now unto him that is able to do exceeding abundantly above all that we ask or think, according to the power that worketh in us,
Ephesians 3:20

We rightly love to harp on God's side in answering prayers captured in those words "exceedingly abundantly above all that we ask or think". When we don't see change, we think it is because God has not done "exceedingly abundantly above all that we ask". God does not answer prayers based on His mood. Answers to prayer involve God's side and man's side for they are "according to the power working in us"! God uses His power within you to answer your prayers. God's ability to answer our prayers is in proportion to His power that is put to work within us. God intervenes in our situation through us as we put His power within us to work.

When we pray, we want the physical material. God does not give us the physical material that we have in mind when we pray. God does not govern physical materials. We do. What God gives to us is the spiritual equivalent in pure power form within our inner man. The power of God within you is what becomes anything that you desire in the physical dimension. Bible Faith takes the power-form of things and changes them to their material equivalent.

We are co-labourers with God and we co-create the manifestation of answered prayers together with God. God works with us through the Holy Spirit depositing power within our inner man. We work with Him by releasing the power from our heart into the world around us through faith. God does not release the power into our circumstances. God works within us, while we work these things that He was worked within us out. God works in (Phil. 2:13), you work out (Phil. 2:12) what He has worked in!

Most of the time we are not conscious that answers to prayer exist within our inner man in power form. This is because our attention is fixed on the realm of our need instead of the realm of God's supply. It is up to you to put that power to work within you. We release that power from within our inner man through spoken words that then transfer it into the mountains, issues and circumstances that stand in our path.

Let's restate what Paul is teaching here:

The riches of God's grace cannot give you someone else's car or wife or job; that's covetousness (Jam. 4:3). You recognize that your need falls within the scope of what the riches of God's grace supplied to you in Christ. So you pray to God.

You are conscious that the answer already exists.

God hears you and places the answer within your inner man as the spiritual substance of power.

God, Man and the answer are all spiritual in nature.

God does not give answers to you in their physical form.

The answer, which already exists, might register in your feelings immediately or take a while to produce feelings but you don't go with the presence or absence of feelings. You go with faith in God's Word.
You then change this answer from its power-form into the form of your need through your faith and actions.

Use the shield of faith

The thief aims to steal this consciousness of resident power from you. He uses arguments in your thoughts to convict you that you received nothing. He needs to make you doubt that the kingdom will produce within you. When this happens, you are to use your shield of faith to release God's Word out of your mouth to quench satan's arguments (Eph. 6:16). The way to do this is to speak God's Word of promise out of your mouth. As you speak the Word of God out of your own mouth, you are causing faith to come (Rom. 10:17). When faith has come, as you continue to speak God's Word, you release the power contained within the Word to release change in our experience.

17

REMOVE HINDRANCES TO FAITH

The Lord Jesus taught a simple but powerful lesson that helps us understand the operation of faith.

For verily I say unto you, That whosoever shall say unto this mountain, Be thou removed, and be thou cast into the sea; and shall not doubt in his heart, but shall believe that those things which he saith shall come to pass; he shall have whatsoever he saith.
Mark 11:23

The law of faith makes sense when you understand the universe of tiny particles.

Though literal mountains look solid and unmoving, housed within it are billions of trillions of sub-atomic particles "running around" with energy. That mountain is vibrating all the time, your eyes are just not designed to see those spaces within it; therefore, you remain convinced it is a solid impenetrable, immovable mountain. The mountain can move! Anything in this material universe, including your house, car and fingernail vibrates. Scientists tell us that colours are waves vibrating at different frequencies. Certain things carry higher vibrations or frequencies that produce effects on the things around you. When you put your pot of soup on your gas burner, the energy supplied from the burner agitates the molecules in your pot of soup and heats it up. Think of the Word of God as a limitless supply of super high frequency vibrations that you can release against any mountain to agitate it, heat it up, move it and alter it.

This universe contains tiny particles that form very large objects. These tiny particles mess with what we think we understand from observing large objects. Scientists have noted that these particles behave differently depending on the observer. They exist as waves until some researcher looks at them and at that very instant they change to particles. In the universe of tiny particles that make up the really big things, nothing is there until you look. We tend to find what we are looking for. Things are busy responding to you even if you cannot immediately see your effect on these things. Consider the case where your thoughts are sending out the vibrations, "I can't find my wallet". The second you develop a firm and completely unshakable I-can't-find-my-wallet conviction, your wallet no longer exist for you to find. A blanket of illusion envelops your vision, thus stopping you from seeing the wallet. Yet, once you permit yourself to move into the I-believe-the-wallet-is-definitely-here version of reality, your belief disintegrates the blanket of illusion and causes the wallet to announce itself to you as you later find it in the place where you had looked several times, confident that it was not there, yet there it was.

The mountain will obey you

When the Lord Jesus said that the mountain would move if we speak to it and doubt not, He was letting us into how this universe is designed by God. When you speak, your words are waves, unseen vibrations that are a form of energy. This sustained energy flowing from your words will vibrate the molecules that make up the "mountain" and move it out of your way. This is one way of understanding the effect of our spoken words on mountains.

Some folks think that anything prefaced with God and completed by the mantra "In Jesus name" qualifies as prayer. Thinking this way, some people pray, "God, please remove this mountain that stands before me which keeps getting bigger day by day in Jesus name" and they are surprised to hear that the devil says "Amen and Amen" to that kind of praying. They are sending out vibrations that establish the mountain rather than move it.

We have the permission and authority from God to move mountains. The moving of mountains involves the release of spiritual power. He leaves it up to us to apply the power, which He makes available in His Word. We are to transmit this power against the mountain. Since we are the ones that the mountain obeys (Lk. 17:6), the logic of scripture leads us to believe that God does not use the power that He supplies.

If we believe the things that we are speaking to the mountain, the mountain will move in accordance with our commands. Faith itself does not create this movement. The mountain moves because the power of God has been applied against it. Faith is how we release that power against the mountain.

For verily I say unto you, That whosoever shall say unto this mountain, Be thou removed, and be thou cast into the sea; and shall not doubt in his

heart, but shall believe that those things which he saith shall come to pass;
he shall have whatsoever he saith.
And when ye stand praying, forgive, if ye have ought against any: that
your Father also which is in heaven may forgive you your trespasses.
Mark 11:23, 25

Praying is built on words and is to follow on from our words. Don't separate your saying from your praying. Praying and saying are both scriptural ways of calling forth and establishing things. Your saying can hinder your praying. If you say one thing and prayer another, your words can move your praying out of the way! We are unprepared to take our place in prayer until we learn to hold fast to the confession of the Word of God.

Many rush into prayer without getting their words to align with God's Word.

When we speak words of command to the mountain, power is released that causes the mountain to move. Specifically, we must not doubt that power is present in our words and that faith is releasing power through our commands. We must not doubt that these commands against the mountain will come to pass. If we doubt that power is present in our words, we release power against our own progress. We empower the mountain to persist. This is the specific doubt that hinders our faith.

Jesus did not say anything about doubting with our brains. If your brain doubts, it is simply doing its job of weighing evidences in the natural world. The brain continually adjusts based on the evidences it receives from the senses. That is purely biological in nature. What Jesus is discussing is not about the brain altering its judgement in line with changes in the environment. Doubt in the heart causes the heart to fail. The heart blocks the release of power therefore the mountain will not move. Both heart doubt and faith operate out of the heart (Rom 10:10). So, if you believe with your heart that your words are working they will work but if you doubt with the heart that your words are working, then you are causing civil war in your own heart and binding your faith! While doubting with the head does not undo the effect of your faith, doubting with the heart will. All types of unbelief are harmful to faith. Unbelief is always treated as evil (Heb. 3:12).

Jesus also lets us know that unforgiveness has the same effect as heart doubt. Unforgiveness stops the moving of the mountain because both doubt in the heart and unforgiveness will operate, so as to resist the effectiveness of your faith. Unbelief and heart-doubt are hindrances to the man side and not the God side. Unforgiveness does not block God from giving because His giving is a function of His grace and not of your faith. Unforgiveness withdraws the effectiveness of your faith.

Faith will work to release the power of God, while either of doubt in the heart or unforgiveness will block the power from being released. It is like a tug of war.

Remove the forces blocking your faith

The Lord Jesus implies that while faith is releasing the power of God's Word, it is possible for unforgiveness to be released at the same time from the heart against someone that has hurt us. When this happens, the unforgiveness that is active in the heart undoes all the beautiful work that faith is doing in releasing power against the mountain. Unbelief is an enemy of effective faith. It works to produce a cancellation of the power released by faith. The net effect is zero or worse. The mountain does not move. Since this is true for unforgiveness, we can understand how it is possible for doubt in the heart to work at the same time as faith. This means that the presence of faith is not the absence of doubt and unbelief. It is possible to be busy applying the correct spiritual principles for moving a mountain but to also be releasing doubt out of your heart at the same time. Jesus says, "If he shall believe … and doubt not".

Let's look at an instance where doubt cancelled out the effectiveness of faith:

And Peter answered him and said, Lord, if it be thou, bid me come unto thee on the water. And he said, Come. And when Peter was come down out of the ship, he walked on the water, to go to Jesus. But when he saw the wind boisterous, he was afraid; and beginning to sink, he cried, saying, Lord, save me. And immediately Jesus stretched forth his hand, and caught him, and said unto him, O thou of little faith, wherefore didst thou doubt? And when they were come into the ship, the wind ceased.
Matthew 14:28-32

Jesus said Peter had little faith, yet with little faith Peter walked on water!

Peter had cornered Jesus into saying, "come". That was all Peter needed in order to walk on water. When Jesus said "Come", He transported the power to walk on water to Peter whose ears fed that power into his heart. Faith came when Peter heard Jesus. Jesus' frame of reality was such that every word flowing out of Jesus was pregnant with the reality of walking on water. When Jesus said, "come", there was enough substance in those words to cause Peter to walk on water. Peter believed that word and his action released that water-walking-power of God's Word. Peter walked on water. That power continued to work once released. Jesus never withdrew that power.

While the power was working, Peter saw the wind that had been blowing all the while and he became afraid. Now he has added the spiritual baggage of fear to the faith that was supplied through his hearing Jesus say, "Come". When Peter yielded to doubt, he blocked the operation of the power that his actions of faith had released for walking on water and the laws of classical physics set in causing him to start to sink. Thus, when Peter focused less on Jesus and His Word, he started to sink. Earlier as he acted on the Word the power released by faith caused him to walk on water.

We give Peter a lot of grief for how he handled walking on water but the truth is that he ultimately walked with Jesus back to the boat. So, we know he recovered in time to actually walk on water!

Beginning to sink

I have not met or heard of people who began to sink. The conditions on a stormy sea would not allow for such. In order to begin to sink it must mean that it is happening in some sort of slow motion and that Peter did not drop like a steel bar into the bottom of the sea. In order to "begin" to sink, two different power sources were acting upon him but in nearly zero effect. This lends itself to the observation that most people do not tend to yield completely to faith or doubt and unbelief. When people yield fully to unbelief, they shut out the power of God from manifesting. If that were what Peter had done in this instance, he would have sunk immediately. When people yield to one or the other at intervals, they have a yo-yo experience. One minute they are walking on water and the next they are starting to sink.

O thou of little faith, wherefore didst thou doubt?
Matthew 14:31b

People who are trained in rescuing those who are drowning at sea know that if it is not well done, the person you are trying to save could end up causing you to drown through their own panic. Jesus was so full of the spiritual substance that caused Him to walk on water that when Peter began to sink, Jesus reached out to grab a drowning man. Jesus immediately reached out to pull Peter out of a stormy sea and released enough power to cause two full-grown men to walk on water. Jesus does not play the blame game. Even when Peter was floundering, Jesus was so highly developed in mercy that He first reached out to catch Peter without any hesitation before explaining to Peter why he was sinking. Hard-hearted people would have first lectured Peter that he was reaping the seeds he had sown through fear.

Jesus acknowledged that God's power was not the variable. He knew that Peter had faith. Jesus had seen Peter demonstrate enough faith to walk on water; therefore, it was not a faith-problem. The variable was doubt.

Jesus pointed out that Peter had added doubting to his faith. Peter doubted because he was afraid. Doubt blocked Peter from continuing to enjoy the power contained within Jesus' statement, "Come". Peter's did not doubt the extent of God's power. He doubted his own ability to keep receiving the continuous miracle of walking on water by faith. He became less conscious that the power once released was working for him in that situation.

Doubt and unforgiveness in the heart act as power blockers and if allowed to work, they block faith's release of the spiritual power of God. Doubt reigns where there is ignorance and uncertainty. You starve your doubt by feasting on the knowledge of the truth of God's Word. You destroy unbelief and reverse a hard heart by believing the Word and using the knowledge of the truth to unlearn all contrary things.

Starve your doubts

And there came a leper to him, beseeching him, and kneeling down to him, and saying unto him, If thou wilt, thou canst make me clean. And Jesus, moved with compassion, put forth his hand, and touched him, and saith unto him, I will; be thou clean. And as soon as he had spoken, immediately the leprosy departed from him, and he was cleansed
Mark 1:40-42

Nothing happened to this Leper until after Jesus had spoken. This leper had likely seen or heard of Jesus healing others but not necessarily a case of leprosy. His doubt derived from centuries of tradition for under the Law of Moses, Jesus would have been forbidden from touching a leper. This leper had doubts in his heart as to whether Jesus would touch him. Even when Jesus touched him, the leprosy did not go because the man's unanswered question placed a ceiling on his ability to receive the power that was resident in Jesus. This doubt was removed when Jesus gave him knowledge. He heard and believed the information that Jesus gave him. The knowledge of the truth set him free from the bondage of ignorance. (Mk. 1:42)

Heart doubt is of two varieties. It manifests as hesitancy because you do not have enough information from God's Word. The cure for that doubt is to gain confidence by saturating your heart with the knowledge of the truth of God's Word. The second variety of doubting comes because we neglect God's Word and let truth that you once knew slip away from you. You might find yourself doubting again. The cure is to start paying attention to the truth in the same way that a waiter would to a paying customer in a posh restaurant. On a further note, Jesus recommends fasting as a cure for unbelief, since it helps increase our awareness of the spirit realm. We find it easier to believe God's supernatural Word (Mt 17:20-21).

Uprooting unforgiveness

and become kind to one another, tender-hearted, forgiving one another, even as God also in Christ forgave you
Ephesians 4:32 (WORRELL)

You are to remember that God has forgiven you in redemption through the blood of Jesus. Therefore, you should choose to walk in the love of God that is within you, in honour of that blood. This is how you deal with unforgiveness. You can uproot the influence of unforgiveness over you by your deciding not to act on thoughts of unforgiveness arising from the flesh. Act on love thoughts flowing from the Word and from your spirit.

If you do not starve unbelief, doubts and unforgiveness, they will feed off you until they become giants in your world. Can you picture the fastest man on earth strapping a big sack of potatoes to his feet while he is running the finals of the 200m at the Olympics? He would no doubt generate a lot of energy to carry that weight while trying to run, but for all his efforts he will hardly make any progress. The sack of potatoes would weigh him down and hinder him from unleashing his true potential. In order to carry that weight while still retaining his speed, he would need to become much bigger. Otherwise, he could offload the sack of potatoes, so as to achieve optimal results. Believers who want to accommodate big doubt, massive unforgiveness, and big unbelief would always need "bigger" faith. Such faith is massively drained with zero achievement. The Christian wants zero doubt, zero unforgiveness and zero unbelief. Then, even a little faith goes a long way. We need less doubt and unbelief, not more faith per se.

The danger of unbelief

Then came the disciples to Jesus apart, and said, Why could not we cast him out? And Jesus said unto them, Because of your unbelief: for verily I say unto you, If ye have faith as a grain of mustard seed, ye shall say unto this mountain, Remove hence to yonder place; and it shall remove; and nothing shall be impossible unto you. Howbeit this kind goeth not out but by prayer and fasting.
Matthew 17:19-21

Jesus' disciples had successfully exercised power over demonic influences while ministering in different cities in Israel (Luke 10:17). These disciples approached the Lord perplexed as to why they failed in this case. Our first instinct is to conclude that they were powerless to deal with the situation at hand. We are quick to blame everything on powerlessness. The Lord Jesus mercifully answered their questions and revealed to them that theirs was a problem of unbelief and not one of lack of power. Their unbelief hindered them from operating in the power of God. The Word says they could (Lk. 10:19). They believed they could not. Unbelief is really a result of what you believe.

By observing circumstances, the disciples were casting out faith instead of casting out the demon. They must have observed the boy appearing dead after they cast out the demon and concluded that their faith failed. This is exactly what the demon did when Jesus finally casted it out (Mk. 9:26). Jesus acted on His faith even when the little boy looked dead (Mk. 9:27).

Jesus basically says that they had unbelief in addition to their faith and when you allow those two coexist in your heart, you create perplexing scenarios.

Unconscious unbelief

The boy's father gives a lot away when he says, "I believe, help my unbelief". He admits to operating in both unbelief and faith simultaneously. Whereas the boy's father knew he had unbelief, the disciples did not know they were in unbelief until they heard Jesus' explanation in response to their question. The disciples had believed enough to lay hands on this boy to be healed and delivered. It was an unconscious form of unbelief. The disciples had not lost the power. Unbelief hinders the flow of God's power. The power was getting released as they commanded manifestation in faith. Unbelief was also cancelling out that power. The net effect was zero healing or deliverance.

Jesus did not put any responsibility on the little boy for his healing. Jesus speaking to His own ministers said, "It is because of your UNBELIEF!" According to Jesus, the predicament was down to the fact that these precious ministers were operating in an unconscious unbelief. A fellow may be walking in unbelief and not know it. Rather than deal with the unbelief, he attributes lack of manifestation to every other conceivable reason under the sun. A minister who is walking in unconscious unbelief might find that he is leading his hearers into unbelief. In most cases, while we are scratching our heads wondering why God has not healed this person or that person after we have done all that we know to do from His Word, God is also concerned that we are leaving people ill.

We need to learn how to minister God's life and power to people instead of blaming them for their lack of faith. They already had enough faith to come to us in the first place! Religion trains people to transfer guilt onto the one who has come to be healed and when they are unable to successfully pin that blame on the seeker, they hinge it on the supposed mysteries of the sovereignty of God. Jesus did not once bring God into the equation when he was answering this question. Jesus holds the mature believers and the ministers responsible.

The sovereignty of God is not so much the issue as is the fact that God has limited Himself to operating on this earth through His body. Jesus in that instance was the available agent through which God could work effectively because Jesus was free from unbelief. Both the Lord Jesus and the disciples had power, both the Lord Jesus and the disciples had faith to release God's power; but while the disciples had unbelief, Jesus had none. Therefore, there was no hindrance to the flow of God's power through Him. The power of God worked once there was a man that knew how to release it.

To their credit the disciples of Jesus did not say to the man, "Let's wait for Jesus before we do anything about this scenario". Someone has said that Pentecostals make bad spiritual policemen because we generally tend to make no "arrests" but wait for "God" to show up to decide in every local case where satan has robbed men.

This boy's father is also to be commended, for he did not receive his son's condition as a lesson from God. He did not conclude after nine anointed disciples had prayed unsuccessfully that it might be a message from God telling him to let things continue as they are. He did not say, "I do not know why God will not heal my son". He said to Jesus, "Your disciples could not heal him". The Lord Jesus did not correct him and say, "Leave this in God's hands and if He thinks that you are deserving He will do something". We should adopt this man's stance more often, if we are to see more demonstrations of the miraculous. We see cold aloofness on God's part, when in fact we should place the responsibility of seeing manifestations of healing on man.

Identifying unbelief

What on earth is unbelief and can we identify it?

We find some clues in Paul's inspired coverage of the birth of Abraham's son Isaac. Abraham wanted to bring forth a miracle son with Sarah, his wife. Even though God had promised this child to them, they took a long time in receiving the birth of this miracle son. Finally, after more than twenty-four years, Abraham received the birth of his miracle son at the age of one hundred years old. In interpreting this, Paul introduces the subject of unbelief.

> *And not being weak in faith, Abraham did not consider his own body, already dead (since he was about a hundred years old), and the deadness of Sarah's womb. He did not waiver at the promise of God through unbelief*
> Romans 4:19-20

Abraham was tempted to base his expectations on the deadness of Sarah's womb as well as his own ageing body. Abraham was aware that his body was ageing. If he were unaware of this, he would be in denial and not in faith! If all we do is consider our limitations, we become more aware of them. This hardens our heart towards the supernatural and weakens faith's tenacity. Weak faith is the end product of shifting our consciousness away from God's Word. Being weak in faith therefore is not about little faith but our mixing of unbelief with faith. Shifting our consciousness away from God's Word leaves us no other option but to become overwhelmed with the things that happen around us in the natural sphere of life.

Abraham could have said, "I am one hundred years old and my wife is now ninety years old, therefore we cannot have a baby." That would be a decision. He would have made perfect sense but would have prevented himself from experiencing God's power. Unbelief decides against God's Word. On the basis of God's promise to him, he could have said, "It is true that I am now one hundred years old and my wife is ninety but according to His promise, praise God we are having our son!" The trouble is not the age, which is simply a measure of the passage of time but the conclusions drawn as a result of our persuasions. An ageing body is not a morally bad thing. It is what you chose to use as your evidence that determines whether or not you are weak in faith. Faith does not deny the circumstances around us; it simply chooses to enforce the alternative experiences locked up in the promises of God.

Unbelief is a way of reasoning against the Word. Its slant is wholly natural. Unbelief can come across as logical and factual but its conclusions deny power from flowing from the spirit into the heart to overwhelm our circumstances. Carnal reasoning is the chief sponsor of unbelief. Whenever you waver as a result of only concentrating on the evidence of the senses, you are in unbelief. Unbelief is a function of what you attend to. If you attend continually to the evidence of the natural world, which in themselves might be perfectly legitimate scenarios, you harden your heart against faith. Your heart softens towards unbelief. To recover from this, you need to remember and consider God's Word more until the Word builds your will and sharpens your reasoning. This strengthens your soul to line up with your spirit. The end product is that your miracle can manifest out of the invisible realm of possibilities.

Apart from staying more in the Word, here are some steps that can help you rise above the hindrances to faith.

Pray in tongues

The mountain goes or stays depending on what you do with doubt (Mk 11:23). After releasing your faith, did you doubt or did you not doubt? If the mountain did not go, it's something to do with your doubts. How do we respond to this challenge of doubt? We doubt because we are less spirit conscious. We have operated our hearts in a way that elevates the soul above the spirit. The cure is to exercise the heart so it reflects the spirit's ascendancy over the soul. When you have your spirit's ascendancy over your soul, you are able to believe with your whole heart. Prayer in tongues does not affect the mountains. It affects you by supplying edification (1 Cor. 14:4). Edification is a long-term change that elevates you above the mess of doubting with the heart. Edification promotes you above doubts. We overdose our understanding with the edification we received through tongues.

Worship & Confession

Worship basically stirs up your awareness of God's presence and His anointing until you are overdosed on His power. It magnifies God to your senses. Spirit-empowered worship causes Christ to be glorified to you. The consciousness of Jesus brings you to a fresh comprehension of the Father. New Testament worship amplifies the presence of God to your soul. You become more aware of spiritual things. The human spirit and the Holy Spirit become more real. When you are conscious of God there is a flow. Worship sweetens our confession of God's Word while dulling us to any feelings of dryness. You will find it helpful if you worship and then follow it up with the confession of God's Word to yourself (Eph. 5:19). You are not changing anything externally per se. You are making God's Word the content of your mind. You are speaking the Word frequently to yourself for as long as it takes. It is like pampering your soul in the sauna of

God's Word.

18

AFTER PRAYER:
WORDS & ACTIONS

And Jesus, immediately knowing in himself that virtue had gone out of him, turned him about in the press, and said, Who touched my clothes?
Mark 5:30

And it came to pass on a certain day, as he was teaching, that there were Pharisees and doctors of the law sitting by, which were come out of every town of Galilee, and Judaea, and Jerusalem: and the power of the Lord was present to heal them.
Luke 5:17

The virtue that went out of Jesus is really referring to the resident power of God that Jesus carried about with Him after He had been anointed with the Spirit of God (Acts 10:38). That power was transferred into people who touched Him or His reaching out to touch them. The touch of faith then released that power to heal and deliver them all. Faith itself did not heal them. Faith released the flow of power that healed them.

The power stored in Jesus flowed when Jesus released it into someone by the laying on of His hands. Some other people also released the power of God resident on Jesus by exercising their faith. For those scenarios, the Lord Jesus says, "Your faith has made you whole". In those instances, you don't find Him speaking to their sickness or disease because the person's faith has already done what Jesus would have done to release that power (Mk 5:34).

And Jesus, immediately knowing in himself that virtue had gone out of him, turned him about in the press, and said, Who touched my clothes? And his disciples said unto him, Thou seest the multitude thronging thee, and sayest thou, Who touched me? And he looked round about to see her that had done this thing
Mark 5:30-32

The woman with the issue of blood was healed without a conscious decision from Jesus. She proved that it was not Jesus per se that healed the sick. Jesus was the container of the power of God. In the ministry of Jesus, it was the power of God that was flowing out of Jesus that healed the sick. Jesus was expert at using his faith to release the flow of power. This woman copied Jesus by using her faith to release the power resident in Jesus, so that she reaped the same manifestations of healing power. Her act of faith placed a demand on the flow of that power and transferred it out of Jesus without needing to get Jesus' permission.

Jesus did not know who touched him. Yet the power of God that flowed out of Him still worked to drive out sickness and disease in that woman. This shows that God is not tackling sickness on a case-by-case basis nor is He taking personal decisions on every single instance of healing.

After prayer, speak the command

Now there was at Joppa a certain disciple named Tabitha, which by interpretation is called Dorcas: this woman was full of good works and almsdeeds which she did. And it came to pass in those days, that she was sick, and died: whom when they had washed, they laid her in an upper chamber. And forasmuch as Lydda was nigh to Joppa, and the disciples had heard that Peter was there, they sent unto him two men, desiring him that he would not delay to come to them. Then Peter arose and went with them. When he was come, they brought him into the upper chamber: and all the widows stood by him weeping, and shewing the coats and garments which Dorcas made, while she was with them. But Peter put them all forth, and kneeled down, and prayed; and turning him to the body said, Tabitha, arise. And she opened her eyes: and when she saw Peter, she sat up.
Acts 9:36-40

Good works are important. Our good works save us before men. Not before God. Tabitha's good works gave her a good standing before people who then sent for Peter, when she could not. Her good works did not raise her from the dead though. She came back to life because of a man that knew how to put God's power to use.

When Tabitha died, Peter was called on the scene. You would find that whenever Jesus took people along with Him in the raising of the dead, He always took Peter (Mk 5:37-43, Lk. 8:51-56). Peter knew from observing Jesus that in such situations not everyone knows how to contribute meaningfully to the reversal of physical death. Peter therefore put everyone out. Though Peter favored kneeling down in prayer, it is not a prayer secret to kneel in prayer. Posture only matters if we believe that it does. It is simply a matter of personality and preference. Find what works for you.

If the content of Peter's prayer had been important, the Lord would have instructed Luke to write it down. Luke wrote down what happened after Peter had prayed.

Tabitha did not rise from the dead after Peter drove everyone out, knelt down, or even prayed.

Tabitha rose from the dead after Peter spoke to Tabitha's body!

This was Jesus' style.

Jesus usually spoke to the dead body.

Damsel, I say unto thee, arise (Mk. 5:41). Lazarus, come forth (John 11:43). Young man, I say unto thee, Arise (Lk. 7:14).

Peter did not ask God to speak to Tabitha's body. Prayer imparted Peter with boldness. Prayer was the beginning and not the end. Now Peter, as a man, had to take charge of that situation by releasing the word of command. The Bible sequence is that even after prayer, we command and then the transmitted power of God in our command works in the natural dimension to cause change, which in this instance reversed death.

Many of us still stop at prayer. We think that after praying we have addressed the issues and that the ball is now in God's court. We expect God to take charge. Peter did not think so. He realized that God has given men with a physical body the charge of this earth, so he spoke to Tabitha's body. Peter's command of faith transported power into Tabitha's body to retain her spirit.

There is a principle involved here. The power of God can be present and its effect not experienced in the physical realm. Peter did something with the power of God. This was the corresponding action to what he believed God for. He spoke out a command. An action in the physical dimension is necessary in order to turn the spiritual substance of God's power into its biological form. Do dead people have a choice in returning to life? We have no way of proving that dead people have no choice in coming back to the body or not. If Tabitha were sick instead of dead, an action on her part would have been necessary to turn the power from a spiritual form to a physical form that can sustain her health. The least action is the action of speaking a command after praying. Peter's prayer stirred up boldness and released power. His command directed the power. His actions released it into Tabitha's body.

Let's consider another instance where prayer is mentioned in the Bible in relation to someone receiving a miracle.

These things said he: and after that he saith unto them, Our friend Lazarus sleepeth; but I go, that I may awake him out of sleep. Then said his disciples, Lord, if he sleep, he shall do well. Howbeit Jesus spake of his death: but they thought that he had spoken of taking of rest in sleep. Jesus therefore again groaning in himself cometh to the grave. It was a cave, and a stone lay upon it. Jesus said, Take ye away the stone. Martha, the sister of him that was dead, saith unto him, Lord, by this time he stinketh: for he hath been dead four days. Jesus saith unto her, Said I not unto thee, that, if thou wouldest believe, thou shouldest see the glory of God? Then they took away the stone from the place where the dead was laid. And Jesus lifted up his eyes, and said, Father, I thank thee that thou hast heard me. And I knew that thou hearest me always: but because of the people which stand by I said it, that they may believe that thou hast sent me. And when he thus had spoken, he cried with a loud voice, Lazarus, come forth. And he that was dead came forth, bound hand and foot with graveclothes: and his face was bound about with a napkin. Jesus saith unto them, Loose him, and let him go.
John 11:11-13, 38-44

Some Greek scholars tell us that what Jesus said was, "Lazarus died". He was reporting a past event to His disciples. Jesus had not gone immediately because the Jews had assassins out for Him. Jesus compared Lazarus' death to sleep from which a man would awaken. We expect sleeping people to wake up. Jesus was not denying that Lazarus had died. Lazarus had been dead for four days. Jesus was painting an inner image of Lazarus' resurrection. Jesus attempted to free the disciple's heart from the fear of death. Fear of death would have enforced the grip of death on Lazarus. He did this so well that the disciples concluded that Lazarus was not dead.

When Jesus got to the tomb, He gave thanks to God that God heard Him always. After Jesus gave thanks to God, Lazarus did not rise up. Lazarus was still in the grave.
Jesus did not tell God to raise Lazarus from the dead.

He did not stop at thanking God in prayer. The Lord Jesus said, "Lazarus, come forth!"

Jesus specifically commanded Lazarus to come forth. Perhaps, if Jesus had not mentioned Lazarus by name and had just looked in the direction of the grave and said, "come forth", all the dead might have responded. The Bible sequence is that we first command and then the transmitted power of God works in the natural dimension. When the Lord Jesus commanded Lazarus to come forth, He was not speaking as God. He spoke as a man on the earth with authority. The words of Jesus transmitted the power of God into the body of Lazarus. Our religious minds thinks that the correct thing is to pray to God asking Him to deal with these issues but this was not the style or practice of the Apostle Peter and the Lord Jesus Christ.

After praying, learn to release commands. Speak to the situation knowing that you have authority as well as precedence from God's Word to act this way. You are following in the footsteps of those who have like precious faith to us. The power to reverse death was present before Peter spoke but it was when the word of command was given that this power was applied to undo the effects of death in Tabitha's body. If you do not believe that you have the right to command the reversal of unwanted situations in the physical dimension, you might find yourself waiting on God to do that which He has not said He will do. He is faithful with the supply of His power. Will you be faithful after prayer to command His power?

The power is not in the office, but in the name

And Peter, fastening his eyes upon him with John, said, Look on us. And he gave heed unto them, expecting to receive something of them. Then Peter said, Silver and gold have I none; but such as I have give I thee: In the name of Jesus Christ of Nazareth rise up and walk. And he took him by the right hand, and lifted him up: and immediately his feet and ankle bones received strength. And he leaping up stood, and walked, and entered with them into the temple, walking, and leaping, and praising God.
Acts 3:4-8

The story of Peter and John's encounter with the man at the beautiful gate is hazardous to religious thinking. Peter and John boldly instructed the guy, "Look on us". Very few folks would recommend this as the opening statement to usher in the miraculous. "Look on us" is not likely the first thing that we would have said and maybe that explains why we often try to counsel people out of issues rather than offering the miraculous.

Peter conversed with the man until he got his attention. He did not say, "Let's pray and see what the Lord wants done". They did not pray at that point. They spoke to the man. Prayer has its place but it is not a replacement for the use and release of faith-filled words. In both the instance of the raising of Tabitha from the dead as well as the healing of the man by the gate beautiful, Peter released a command. Speaking words of command is more fundamentally important in these matters than prayer itself is. Follow your prayer with spoken commands, which apply the power of God that is available. Even after that command, the man was still not visibly healed. It was immediately after Peter reached out to lift the man that the man's healing was manifest. Actions caused power to change into physical manifestation. Healing was the launching pad for these guys to then minister the Word. Today, after healings we close the meeting thinking the job is done. Peter did not think that everything leads up to the healing. The healing sets the stage for the Word. After people are healed they still need the Word.

The command was directed at the man. The principle is that the power that was given to the apostles was released through faith and the spoken words of our command. You will notice that the command does not really ask God to do anything. Faith in the name of Jesus commands manifestation of power.

And his name through faith in his name hath made this man strong, whom ye see and know: yea, the faith which is by him hath given him this perfect soundness in the presence of you all.
Acts 4:16

Peter said that it was the name of Jesus and faith in that name that healed the man. He did not say it was his office as Apostle that did it. We do not use the name of Jesus like something magical or as some would use an amulet. We are to develop knowledge of its power through the Word of God. We should listen to the Father whisper to us the power that He has invested in that name and as we listen to him within, faith arises from that knowledge.

Peter gave to this man through the name of Jesus. He gave

because he knew the degree to which he had what he had. Our consciousness of the name of Jesus grows. There is no variation in the name itself. It is equal in ability in all spheres of human existence and to all men but there is obviously a variation in effectiveness in using that name to release power due to the development of the one using it. Some believers are better at using the name than other believers because their awareness of the name as well as their consciousness of sonship is higher than what some other believers have comprehended.

This means that the use of the name of Jesus depends on each believer. It's not that there are two names or that the name is more powerful with some people. The name is constant and never diminishes in power but the one using it varies. The demon does not need to have confidence that the name will work. Thus we don't remind the demon about anything nor do we need to school it in the Word. Our task is to meditate intensely and extensively on the glory of the name of Jesus and keep watering the seed of revelation. We do this over a period until that name merges into our daily life. As you do this, you are supplying enough transformation to your soul and rescuing your imagination from indifference to that mighty name. Through this process, Christ is gaining access to your mind and you have the bucket to dip with into your spirit river to unleash the power of God that heals, delivers and sets free.

In the Hebrew psyche, a name is not just the sound attached to a thing for identification. It is a way of demonstrating the authority, nature and relationship of that thing to us. To use the name of Jesus in a situation means to unveil His nature into the situation at hand. We use that name knowing that He has come down from heaven as us. We fully anticipate He will extend His influence out from within us because Christ in us is the secret of the New Testament. Functioning in His name means a conscious yielding to His presence and power within you because you trust his indwelling presence to overcome all and to bring all things into subjection.

Why was this man not healed prior to that day? God was not causing a delay. It took Peter a while to realise that it was up to him to release the command that unleashed the faith which then released the power. The typical Christian does not release commands in the name of Jesus. Most do not believe that the name has been given for the believer's use to meet every need. The mentality that most church people have is akin to, "Heavenly Father you have all power and I know that you have perfect knowledge to use that power, please use the power to bring about this change or the other and we will wait while you do it. In Jesus' name Amen". When Peter spoke out the Word of command, the power of God was transported so to speak, into the paralyzed limbs of this dear man who had begged all his life. Peter does not stop there.

He took the man by his right hand (don't you just love the precision and detail of Dr. Luke?)

Peter then lifted the man up!

It was as Peter lifted the man up that the man's feet and ankle bones received strength. The action did not generate power, it released the power that was already present his indwelling presence.

This man was healed as soon as Peter spoke the word of command. He was not walking yet though he was healed. It was when the man allowed Peter to lift him up that they both supplied the corresponding action that completed the miracle. Until they both supplied corresponding action, there was a delay between the healing that had already occurred and the enjoyment of it in the natural plane.

God had left the matter in Peter's hands. He had commanded this man to walk in the name of Jesus but in spite of all of Peter's bravado, the man was apparently not yet benefitting from a healed leg. If that man was not walking it was not down to God but up to the man and Peter. You are to demonstrate the corresponding action that is required to complete the process of faith. Peter needed to understand how to bring God's will to pass. From the "Lord's prayer" (Mt. 6:10), we know that if God's will is not done, earth remains unlike heaven. It is not God that does His own will on earth; it is men who live in a physical flesh and blood body. When Peter spoke the command, God's power was transmitted. You can liken this to broadcasts from a satellite station. Usually you have to switch on your TV, the TV station cannot do that for you. You don't see television programming appear on your TV screen by magic. That action of switching on the TV and selecting a station completes the transmission cycle that allows you enjoy the TV broadcast. When Peter lifted the man up, he effectively helped the man "switch on" the power of God that had previously been transported into that man by Peter's command of faith.

It was not Peter's apostolic office, personal holiness or charismatic personality that healed this man. It was faith and the power of God released through the use of the name of Jesus. We receive the new birth through the name of Jesus today, for there is salvation in no other name (Acts 4:12). We receive this salvation by faith (Eph. 2:8), so the two ingredients are available but are we? God makes power abundantly available but we must believe that in our day, the principles for the release of power are still the same. In the name of Jesus, you are to command the release of power and then as needed you are to act in ways that complete the full cycle of power that is at your disposal.

Speaking the Word is God's outstretched hands

And now, Lord, behold their threatenings: and grant unto thy servants, that with all boldness they may speak thy word, By stretching forth thine hand to heal; and that signs and wonders may be done by the name of thy holy child Jesus. And when they had prayed, the place was shaken where they were assembled together; and they were all filled with the Holy Ghost, and they spake the Word of God with boldness.
Acts 4:29-31

We can learn a lot from the content of this prayer. It is a prayer for boldness to speak the Word, which really results in a fresh anointing of power. When they prayed they were filled with the Holy Spirit and they spoke the Word of God with boldness. This prayer caused them to be filled with the spirit. People that are full of the Spirit speak the Word of God boldly. Folks who speak unbelief after prayer do so because they are not filled with the Spirit. The pattern is that men are filled with the Spirit as a result of which they speak the Word of God boldly and this draws upon the manifest power of God.

There are two sides to the operation of spiritual power to bring about change on the earth. Power must first be generated and afterwards power must be used. God has given man the authority on this earth. The incarnation gives concrete proof that God best affects the earth through a man living on the earth. This is why God had to become a man on this earth in order for salvation to be a possibility. God's ability works best in an incarnational way.

Those disciples prayed that they be enabled to speak God's Words with great boldness, "by stretching forth your hands to heal". These disciples were not asking for boldness to speak God's Word to God. It was boldness to speak the Word of God to men. The principle contained within their prayer is that we are speaking the Word and the spoken word is releasing the power. This is the way that God works with us.

The outstretched arm of God is not an arm dangling in the clouds. It means manifestations of divine power. The truth is that the Word of God streaming out of our mouths become the outstretched arm and power of God that heals. When we speak the Word of God, we are co-labouring with Him. We are stretching out God's hands. We are not stretching out God's hands by speaking the Word to God but by speaking His Word to others. Our boldness in speaking God's Word out of our mouths is the way we stretch out God's hands. God does not determine when His arm is out-stretched or not. We do.

Long time therefore abode they speaking boldly in the Lord, which gave testimony unto the Word of his grace, and granted signs and wonders to be done by their hands.
Acts 14:3

Paul was speaking boldly for the Lord and the Lord confirmed the message of His grace by enabling them to do miraculous signs and wonders. The power was released as they spoke boldly. As they were filled with the Spirit, they spoke the Word of God boldly, therefore, the anointing was in strong flow. There is a relationship between staying full of the Spirit, speaking the Word boldly and manifestations of God's power.

19

KEEP APPLYING THE POWER OF GOD

We can learn more about prayer and the power of God from the story of the birth of John the Baptist.

There was in the days of Herod, the king of Judaea, a certain priest named Zacharias, of the course of Abia: and his wife was of the daughters of Aaron, and her name was Elisabeth. And they were both righteous before God, walking in all the commandments and ordinances of the Lord blameless. And they had no child, because that Elisabeth was barren, and they both were now well stricken in years.
Luke 1:5-7

These are not fables. Luke mentions the names of reigning kings in order to help any good student of secular history fix the time frame of these events.

When Luke says that Zechariah and Elizabeth were blameless,

he does not mean that they were sinless. It means that when they took a false step, they got back in line using the provisions of a bleeding sacrifice in that day. They walked with God by faith and just like Abraham, it was accounted to them as righteousness. It is possible to be righteous before God, walk in all the commandments and ordinances of God and still be barren without children. Religious people like to think that those who would have child bearing issues or face challenges in life will be the pimps, the drug peddlers or the mafia. The Bible shows it is not so black and white! They were not barren because they were worse sinners than all other people on the earth. It was a consequence of living in a fallen world.

And the whole multitude of the people were praying without at the time of incense. And there appeared unto him an angel of the Lord standing on the right side of the altar of incense. And when Zacharias saw him, he was troubled, and fear fell upon him. But the angel said unto him, Fear not, Zacharias: for thy prayer is heard; and thy wife Elisabeth shall bear thee a son, and thou shalt call his name John.
Luke 1:10-13

The angel Gabriel confirmed to Zechariah that his prayers were heard!

This righteous couple had released the power of God as a result of prayers they had prayed in the past (Jam. 5:16). Zechariah was in faith when he prayed the prayer that the angel referred to for the Bible teaches that we first receive in the invisible realm through our believing and then have manifestation later (Mk. 11:24). The angel was commissioned to make Zechariah hear that God had heard his prayers. By the time that the angel got through, Zechariah was a broken man who no longer believed as he once did concerning his having a son. With the passage of time and the delay in manifestation of a son, Zechariah had become much older and his hope was now dead. Whereas he operated in faith in the past, he was now prone to operating in unbelief. The angel was God's way of hooking the answer onto Zechariah.

If he had just prayed for a child that day with doubt and unbelief, his doubt would have cancelled out his praying. On the day Gabriel showed up, Zechariah was more likely to pray out unbelief than faith. He would not have prayed because he believed that he had received before praying. If his hope was still intact at the point that Gabriel delivered the news, he should have danced a jig for joy. The angel brought the answer. Zechariah was the human whose heart God needed in order to manifest that baby on earth.

Don't cancel out your prayer

And Zacharias said unto the angel, Whereby shall I know this? for I am an old man, and my wife well stricken in years.
Luke 1:18

Gabriel said, "Thy prayer is heard". Zechariah's prayer had been answered! Zechariah had set a principle in motion at some time in the past, when his praying had released the power of God. Zechariah was unaware that his answer was already released in the unseen realm. The fact that Zechariah could not see it does not mean that the power was not working. My opinion is that Zechariah's unbelief was about to decommission Gabriel's angelic assignment. He might go to the grave without ever having the manifestation of the baby that was already his! This is why Gabriel had to act quickly. The mercy of God was trying to solve the puzzle called Zechariah. He had to be stopped from keeping his wife in a state of barrenness. Since Gabriel struck Zechariah dumb, it would appear that angels have some latitude when sent on errands. Zechariah's prayers had commissioned

Gabriel to see to the birth of John. Gabriel moved to stop Zechariah from using the words of his mouth like a pesticide to kill the manifestation of the answer, for death and life are in the power of the human tongue (Prov. 18:21). If the angel had not acted, Zechariah's unbelief would have cast out the angel's ministry. God used the Angel to plant the answer deep within Zechariah's heart. The baby was planted in unseen form into Zechariah's heart.

Zechariah had not yet said, "Forget it Gabriel, given the age of my wife and I, we are so old that we will not have a child". He was obviously warming up towards making that kind of declaration from his heart. He had said enough in Gabriel's presence to set off spiritual alarms. Gabriel does not have the power or authority to override the words of a human being; therefore, his best line of action is to stop them being said. The situation was still recoverable. God needs your heart in order to manifest the answer in your life. It is not magic. It is the creative ability of the human heart.

Zechariah persisted in unbelief in the angel's presence. God was protecting the birth of John. The intervention of the angel hindered Zechariah from architecting more pain for his family. Mercy prevented Zechariah from reaping the poison of his unbelief. If unchecked, He could have spoken more unbelief thereby crossing a threshold that destroyed his ability to father a child. His words would have poisoned his heart to cause failure.

And it came to pass, that, as soon as the days of his ministration were accomplished, he departed to his own house. And after those days his wife Elisabeth conceived, and hid herself five months, saying,
Luke 1:23-24

Though the prayer had been answered and Gabriel had taken steps to guarantee that Zechariah would not poison his own harvest, Elizabeth was still not pregnant! Zechariah had to go home to his wife before any pregnancy could manifest. Though the angel said that Zechariah's prayer was answered, Zechariah and Elizabeth could still die childless. Zechariah had to act on the angel's announcement, get up from the place of prayer, go home to his wife and make a baby with her. Zechariah did not need more prayer or angelic conversations. The best prayer was the action of intimacy with his wife to complete the cycle of power that was already set in motion. Power had to change to baby form. The heart was producing action in Zechariah!

Sometimes we need to combat the unbelief of others. Consider this passage carefully.

Combating residual unbelief

And he cometh to Bethsaida; and they bring a blind man unto him, and besought him to touch him. And he took the blind man by the hand, and led him out of the town; and when he had spit on his eyes, and put his hands upon him, he asked him if he saw ought. And he looked up, and said, I see men as trees, walking. After that he put his hands again upon his eyes, and made him look up: and he was restored, and saw every man clearly. And he sent him away to his house, saying, Neither go into the town, nor tell it to any in the town.
Mark 8:22-26

This story of Jesus and the blind man at Bethsaida is the only instance we have in the whole of the New Testament where Jesus laid hands on a guy twice in ministering to him. It is also the only instance where Jesus asked the one receiving ministry if he saw any manifestations yet! This is unusual in the ministry of Jesus. It is worth our meditation and study.

Those that brought the blind man believed in the power that

flowed from touching Jesus or being touched by him. In order to minister the release of the power of God against the man's blindness, Jesus removed the blind man from a town whose culture stirred the response of unbelief. Then Jesus laid hands on him. This man had partial manifestation of healing at Jesus' first touch.

And he sent him away to his house, saying, Neither go into the town, nor tell it to any in the town.
Mark 8:26

We don't experience instant manifestation of answers to prayers because there are other factors that come into play after we have received the answer in power form spiritually in the unseen realm. The cumulative unbelief of others could affect us in ways that we are unaware of except we become established in staying focused on receiving and releasing God's power. There are so many answers to prayers that God has said an emphatic "Yes" to but men don't understand that there are principles governing manifestation. So as to trigger full manifestation of healing, Jesus combated the residual unbelief that was still operating in the man. Finally, Jesus continued to apply the power of God by laying hands a second time.

After this blind man had obtained full manifestation, Jesus gave him three instructions,

Go home. Do not go into town. Do not tell anyone in town.

Two of those instructions had to do with the town. That town had an effect on the man.

Jesus was not trying to be anti-social when He told this man not to go back into town but to go home straight away. Certainly, Jesus did not tell this to everyone that received healing through

His ministry. I believe that Jesus was not banning this man from ever going into town for the rest of his life. The unbelief in town at that stage of his life would have caused him to neglect the healing power of God that was at work in his body. Jesus was protecting this guy until the power affected him more than the unbelief in that town. When you believe the damaging words of others, their words settle in your heart and your heart produces the negative things they have spoken. Your heart is that powerful!

The town in question was the town of Bethsaida (Mk 8:22) Bethsaida had witnessed many miracles by Jesus but they remained hardened towards Jesus. This kind of hardness of heart is referred to as an evil heart of unbelief (Mt. 11:21). The advanced unbelief of the town would pressure away the mercy of God. Unbelief is not conducive for the release of power.

Jesus dealt with advanced unbelief in two ways. He threw out those who are highly developed in unbelief, so they would not hinder those who want to receive from God. When the unbelieving ones were the overwhelming majority, Jesus led the man out of the town of Bethsaida, in order to dislodge the man from the grip of unbelief (Mk 8:23).

Persevering in prayer

Did Jesus lay hands twice because God had not heard him the first time?

After Jesus laid hands on the blind man the first time, the man confirmed that he had partial sight. God's power was already released into his body and had caused partial manifestation. Therefore, God had already answered with power. It would appear that power manifests in bursts and not all at once. When Jesus laid hands a second time that act could not have been directed at God again. Enough unbelief was present in the man to hinder full manifestation but not to cancel out the power of God. Hence the man had partial manifestation. Jesus was combating the resistance of unbelief. The devil had access to enforce partial sight through the residual unbelief of the town in the guy. Jesus used the laying on of hands to apply the power again into the body of the man in doses until there was complete manifestation in the physical.

Jesus could have chosen to only lay hands once. In that case, power that had been released would continue to work until over time the partial manifestation matures into a full manifestation. During that process, the blind man would have had to vigorously combat the effect of the unbelief of others in that town by himself. The complete manifestation would come as he kept unbelief away, so that unbelief did not shackle the power that was already at work. This man was in a fragile state where the unbelief in others could trigger the residual unbelief in him. This would cause him to release power against the healing process. This was why Jesus told him not to go into town. It was this unbelief that Jesus used laying on of hands the second time to withstand. This caused the manifestation to go to completion. Perseverance in prayer takes a stand against unbelief and all of satan's tricks. The perseverance of prayer is not directed at God to get Him to move more quickly. If God were slow, where would you generate enough power to hasten him anyway?

Jesus was combating the residual unbelief of Bethsaida in the man. It is one thing to live in a town that openly promotes unbelief but more damaging if some of its slant is lodged within you. When we act in unbelief, our heart releases power that hinders our spiritual growth and increase. Jesus did all He could to help the guy operate beyond the limitations of unbelief imposed by the town. He was not doing this to force God's hands. The power of God was at work in the man but the manifestation of healing was not yet complete. His healing manifestation was partial at that stage. If Jesus had not ministered to the guy this way, it is likely the guy would have headed back into town, heard the old arguments, poisoned his heart and yielded ground to the adversary. Whatever little manifestation of healing he had seen up till that time would have been handcuffed by unbelief.

The guy was at liberty after receiving the full manifestation of his healing, to have gone to the town. In the town, he would have found himself outnumbered and before long, he would be entertaining old beliefs and ideologies. These ideologies would set up resistance to the power of God, which had been released into his body by the laying on of Jesus' hands. Jesus wanted this guy to go home and develop some confidence in the power of God. He wanted him to become accustomed to seeing himself healed.

Praying scripturally in line with God's Word releases the power of God contained within His Word. That power continues to work, no matter what symptoms show up in your experience. Rather than responding in unbelief, you can rest in the fact that the power continues to work in spite of these contradictory evidences.

Greek experts tell us that the Greek word translated "says" in Mark 11:23 is the present continuous tense. Thus, we continue to command the mountain to go. We boldly command these things knowing that a stream of power follows our stream of words. We should continue to use the words of our command and our actions to apply the power of God, until full manifestation comes.

Here is a Psalm that should bless you:

If the Lord's song is in your heart ,
it will flow out of your mouth,
for the night prevails only when the mouth does not release the heart in
praise.
In the midst of adversity, let the tide of praise arise in your heart
Even when it seems that the dark clouds do gather.
let the river of God's light gush forth
and see the deliverance of God.
Sing praise unto the Lord, now and do not defer it to tomorrow
But right now, let praise cause you to soar unto the higher plane.
Sing unto the Ancient of days, the lofty and Mighty One
He has brought light and immortality to light through the gospel
So, sing out of your heart, through your own mouth
For it is right, yea it is right to praise the Father of glory
Let your praying lead up to praise and stay in praise for that is also right!

* 9 7 8 0 9 5 7 5 6 7 7 4 0 *